TWITTER FOR WRITERS

Rayne Hall

TWITTER FOR WRITERS

TWITTER FOR WRITERS

Rayne Hall

CONTENTS

Introduction

Writers need different things from Twitter than 'normal' people.

As a writer, you'll use Twitter to meet colleagues, connect with readers, invite reviews, carry out research, improve your writing, develop networks, gain insight, conduct market studies, build your platform, create buzz for your stories, and sell your work.

Twitter is perfect for writers. It's easy to learn, gives you full control of your network, takes less time than other social media, and doesn't bombard you with flashing pop-ups or distracting invitations to play Candy Crush.

You can use Twitter as a professional tool without wasting your precious writing time – but be warned, Twitter can be addictive. In this book, I'll show you how to use Twitter efficiently and to get the greatest benefits in the shortest time.

"My favourite social network is Twitter. Best interactions, least waste of time."
- Rayne Hall

At the time of writing, I have over 52,000 followers, mostly weird and wonderful writers, and fans of my fiction. Most are real, engaged people who read my tweets and interact, not fake followers and automated accounts. They're also the kind of people who are interested in my books. Some authors have more followers than I – but few have the same quality. The quality of my Twitter 'platform' astonishes marketing experts who sometimes ask me how I do it.

Building this platform took only two years, largely by trial and error, finding out what worked and what did not. By adopting the successful strategies and skipping the mistakes, you can reach similar results even faster.

In this book, I'll show you step by step how you can achieve Twitter success.

I've invented two fictitious writers – Suzie who writes vampire romance novels, and Franco who has published a non-fiction book about dog training – as examples. Adapt my suggestions to suit you. You're the CEO of your Twitter; I'm only the consultant.

You may be new to Twitter, just trying the first steps. Or you may have used Twitter for a while, but aren't really getting anywhere and want to try another approach. You may even be a veteran, looking for advanced techniques to build a platform and promote your books.

For most chapters, I've used this structure: The Basics – What Not To Do – Advanced Strategies - Mistakes I've Made and Learnt From. Read the sections that are relevant for your level and for what you want to achieve. If you're a Twitter novice, stick to The Basics and don't let the Advanced Strategies overwhelm you. As a seasoned Twitter user, you can skip The Basics and try the Advanced Strategies. If you want a laugh, read the sections about my mistakes.

You can also dip into and out of this book to get the guidance you want right now. The early chapters give the practical essentials; the middle chapters are for when you want to achieve something specific, such as holding a TwitterParty and finding reviewers for your book, while the chapters near the end are more entertaining.

Like everything on the internet, Twitter keeps changing. Much of what I taught in a 'Twitter for Writers' class a year ago is already out of date. By the time you read this book, some details may no longer apply, but the foundation is here for you to build on.

The cartoon illustrations are by several artists, mostly by Hanna-Riikka who you can follow on Twitter (@DoNichiArt). While you're at it, you can follow me, too (@RayneHall). Tweet me that you're reading this book, and I'll follow you back.

See you on Twitter,

Rayne

CHAPTER 1: CREATING YOUR PROFILE

Go to Twitter.com. If you have an account, log in, and improve it with these tips.

If you're new, create an account. For this, you'll need to provide some personal details and an email address. You'll be asked to follow some big organisations and famous people before you're allowed to proceed. Just click some at random. You can unfollow them later.

THE BASICS

Don't worry about getting things perfect at this stage. If you change your mind about something, you can make changes.

Full Name and User Name

Both your 'Full Name' and your 'User Name' show up frequently and play an important part in your branding and promotion.

I recommend you use your pen name (the author name of your books) for both. This will help a lot with book marketing, search engine optimisation and such. You may not care about those things yet, but one day they may become tremendously important. Securing your pen name as your User Name now will help you sell books in the future.

For the Full Name, use it exactly as you use it for your books. Let's say you write under the pen name Suzie Scrybe. Then you would use Suzie Scrybe as your Full Name on Twitter – not Suzie Z. Scrybe, S. Scrybe or Miss Scrybe.

For the User Name, pick your pen name as well. However, this time you can't use spaces. Suzie Scrybe is @SuzieScrybe. On Twitter, your user name is always preceded by the '@' symbol.

If your pen name is already taken (that's quite possible), see if you can add punctuation marks. For example, Suzie's user name may be @Suzie_Scrybe or @SuzieScrybe_. You could also add a word, for example @SuzieScrybeBook.

Long pen names are problematic, because Twitter allows only 15 letters for a user name. If you write under the name Clarabella Dorothea Watkins-Himmelreich, you may have to limit your user name to @Himmelreich.

Password

Pick something other people can't guess – not the title of your book. The ideal Password is long and includes punctuation marks and numbers, for example *))King989Arthur((* or *^&3Little^&3Dipper*. Don't use the same Password you use for online banking or other social media.

Write it down somewhere you can access it, but not where hackers can. Change it several times a year.

If you ever suspect your account has been hacked, change the Password at once.

Profile Picture

Your Profile Picture is called an 'avatar' ('avi' for short). Upload one as soon as you create your account. Unless you have a picture, other Twitter users will hold you in contempt or suspect you to be not a real person but a robot. If you don't have a picture that's quite right, upload whatever you have at hand now. You can change it later.

The most effective avatar is a portrait of yourself.

If you don't like to display your photo, use a drawing or painting. Go to OCAL (Open Clipart Library) search 'woman face' or 'man face', pick one that looks a bit like you, download it, and upload it as your Twitter profile picture. OCAL pictures are copyright-free. The drawback is that someone else could be using the same picture.

You could also get an artist to paint an 'artist's impression' of you. This can be realistic or a cartoon. Use intense colours, not pastels. Perhaps someone in your family or circle of friends can do it for you for free. Or you can hire a cartoonist or illustrator, either a hobbyist, an aspiring professional or a professional. Expect to pay between $5 and $50. You can then use the same picture for other purposes, such as your Facebook profile and your Amazon Author Central page.

Don't use a full-body picture, or a picture showing you with hubby, pet or other people. The profile pic will be displayed so small, anything more than the head doesn't work.

A portrait that reflects your genre is best - unless you write erotica. Then it's best to avoid anything sexy, or Twitter users will mistake you for a porn spammer.

If you have books published, consider uploading the cover of your most important book instead of a picture of yourself. This creates potentially huge exposure for your cover, and your followers will see that cover so often that subconsciously they perceive it as a bestselling book. However, the Twitter Profile Picture is square and small. I recommend creating a new picture with a square-cropped part of the cover picture, and the book title pasted into it. Ask a digital design-savvy friend to do this for you. The drawback is that every tweet you send will look like an advertisement, and most people are fed up with seeing advertising everywhere.

Profile Text

Fill in the profile text. Definitely fill in the profile text. That's how people will identify you as an interesting person whose tweets they want to read. You have up to 160 characters.

Don't waste the words on meaningless drivel, and don't try to be overly clever. Use words which will help like-minded people (and readers!) find you.

I recommend you simply say what you write. This will help a lot with marketing and promotion. Use the combination of 'Writer' or 'Author' and your genre(s) or subgenres, for example, 'Paranormal Romance Author'. These three words are all you need. They'll serve you well on Twitter. People who're interested in paranormal romance will find you - and this is your main aim on Twitter.

You can also add search words, based on your interests and what you will tweet about. I recommend using words related to your novels, with or without #hashtags. (More about hashtags in Chapter 6.)

Paragraph breaks don't work in the profile text.

Here are examples:

Rayne Hall
Author & editor of fantasy & horror. Writer's Craft books: Writing Fight Scenes, Writing About Magic, Writing Scary Scenes, Writing Dark Stories & more.

Suzie Scrybe
Suzie Scrybe is a paranormal romance author who loves reading and writing about vampires.

Franco Folly
Author of 'The Zen of Dog Training' & 'Train Your Dog at Home - The Buddhist Way'. #dogs #puppies #buddhism #pets

Notifications

Every time someone follows, favourites, tweets or retweets you or a tweet you were mentioned in, Twitter sends you an email, which soon becomes a nuisance. Twitter also emails you with information about services you can buy. To avoid getting inundated with junk emails, do this:
click the cogwheel symbol at the top. Click 'Settings', click 'Notifications'. Uncheck every Notification. You can change the settings later if you wish.

WHAT NOT TO DO

For your profile picture, avoid using cute animals. Thousands of people on Twitter use pictures of cats and dogs; people won't be able to tell you apart. Use animal pictures in your tweets instead.

Also stay away from pictures of objects, especially typewriters, piles of books, quills and book pages shaped into hearts: so many writers use those as their profile picture, you'll just get lost among many.

Some people use complex code to create Twitter avatars that change, rotate or flash, in hopes of getting attention – but the result looks like annoying advertising, and people hate it.

Don't waste your profile text on useless drivel such as 'If you want to find out about me, read my tweets' or '160 characters is not enough to express who I am'.

Some people's profile text says 'This is the official Twitter account of...' pretending that they're celebrities. You'll become a laughing-stock if you do.

Don't reveal personal information in your profile text.

Don't brag in your profile text. 'Bestselling Author' comes across as hyperbolic and desperate. The genuine bestselling authors don't use such claims.

ADVANCED STRATEGIES

You can change your profile text at any time. The avatar can be changed, too, but not from every device.

In the fast-moving world of Twitter, people will spot your avatar before they notice your name. This is how they recognise you. The familiarity of your avatar is a huge advantage, so avoid changing it.
If you want to experiment with different avatars, do it at the early stages, before you have many followers and before people are accustomed to associating a particular picture with you.

If your branding strategy involves specific colours – perhaps all your book covers are pink – then it can be a good idea to make pink the dominant colour of your avatar. You can further the visual brand recognition by using the same picture for all social media accounts and your website.

You can add further visual elements to your profile, for example, add a 'header' picture and select or create a background wallpaper. Many writers choose their book covers for the wallpaper and click 'tile' so the same picture is repeated over and over. However, these will not be viewed as much as your avatar, and you can skip them if you want to save time.

If you enjoy changing pictures around frequently, play with your header and wallpaper, but keep your avatar consistent.

If you are interested in SEO (search engine optimisation) include your pen name as part of your profile text. 'Suzie Scrybe is a paranormal romance author.' This may look odd if it's directly under your user name, but it helps with search engine optimisation.

Another way to boost SEO is to change the profile text frequently by adding, removing and rearranging words.

However, for the average author, SEO is not a major concern, you may not want to bother.

MISTAKES I MADE AND LEARNT FROM

When I started, I chose an avatar based on the cover of my dark epic fantasy novel Storm Dancer, which I wanted to promote at the time.

STORM
DANCER

Since the cover features a man, people assumed that Rayne Hall was male, and were startled to learn that I'm female. Many imagined that the bloke on the cover was Rayne Hall, and some women tried to flirt.

The book cover as avatar also looked like an advertisement instead of a real person.

After a year, I wanted to change the picture. But by now, I had acquired a huge following who recognised my avatar, and with it an enormous visual brand recognition. I didn't want to throw that advantage away.

Another year passed, during which I gained yet more followers and more brand recognition, and I wished I had changed the avatar long ago. The longer I waited, the more I had to lose.

Eventually, I decided to just do it. Now I'm using this picture:

It's an artist's impression (by Fawnheart) of what I look like, and it's in my brand colours of blue and turquoise, similar to the cartoons and the Writer's Craft book covers. If you look closely, you can see that she painted half of me 'undead', a clever allusion to the kind of stories I write, although this detail is not noticeable at the size normally seen on Twitter.

To smooth the transition, I tweeted for a couple of weeks that I would soon have a new avatar, using the blue picture as an attachment. After the change, I tweeted several times, *I've changed my avatar. New picture, same person, still real*, and attached the old one.

I tweeted these so often that some of my regular followers got bored with the announcement – but others still were confused by the change.

CHAPTER 2: TWEETING

Posts on Twitter are very short – 140 characters or less. This is good, because it allows you to deal with everything in just a few words. You can share news, promote your book, ask questions, comment on discussion threads and reply to fans, and it just takes a few seconds.

Twitter posts are called 'updates' or 'tweets'.

THE BASICS

To send a tweet, click on the quill symbol at the top of your page. Type your message.

Hit 'tweet' to send it. Now, everyone who follows you can see your tweet in their timeline (that's their inbox). This doesn't mean they'll all read it. But they may.

If you've used more than 140 characters, it won't send. Shorten. If necessary, use abbreviations and chatspeak (u = you, 4 = for, & = and, lol = lots of laughter/laughing out loud) - these are not considered stylish, but they're acceptable.

Go ahead and send a few tweets now. Don't be frightened. Twitter is such a fast-moving medium that any 'mistakes' you make will be ignored or forgotten.

Jane Austen says:
"It is a truth universally acknowledged that long sentences don't fit into tweets."

IDEAS FOR TWEETS

1. Introduce Yourself

If you're still feeling your way on Twitter, it's endearing if you are honest. Post something along these lines:

I'm new to Twitter. Any other vampire fiction lovers out there?

Twitter newbie here. I want to follow people who talk about books or vampires. Who's interested?

Hi, I'm Suzie Scrybe and I'm new to Twitter. I love reading and vampires. Do you want to connect?

2. What are you doing right now?

This kind of chatty tweet is popular. People like it because it shows you're a real person, not an automated account.

Examples:

Wet, cold, blustery weather. I'm staying indoors, drinking cappuccino with cardamom. Lovely.

I'm experimenting a new bread recipe. Wholemeal with walnuts and thyme. It's baking now and it smells heavenly.

I've cleaned my bathroom! Really. First time in six months.

Don't tweet non-stop every detail of your life – your followers aren't interested in your daily breakfast menu and digestive actions – but it's a good idea to post chatty status updates now and then.

3. Tweet About Your Likes

My favourite [insert genre] book is [insert title]. Yours?

My favourite movie is [insert title]. I've watched it [insert number] times already. Who else has seen it?

I love [insert animal species]. They're so [insert adjective].

4. Tweet About Your Writing

Share what you're working on now. These tweets will appeal to other writers. You may want to use the hashtag #amwriting, so other writers can find you. (More about connecting with other writers in Chapter 13.)

I'm writing the third chapter of my new vampire romance novel. The fight scene is difficult. #amwriting

I'm trying to write a love scene. I want to create tension, but not erotic. Any advice? #amwriting

Yay! I've completed the first draft of my vampire romance novel and sent it to my critique partners. #amwriting

5. Tweet About Your Book's Subject Matter

What are your books about? Tweet about these topics – not about the books themselves. For example, Suzie who writes vampire romance and Franco who writes about dog training might tweet:

I'm trying out vampire-style make-up for tomorrow's party. Pale foundation, dark eyeshadow. What kind of lipstick, do you think?

I loved the Twilight vampire films the first time I watched them, but not the 2nd. Has anyone else had this reaction?

Two of my dogs love riding in the car. But the third (dachshund) is terrified. I wonder why? Any advice?

It makes me angry when people buy dogs like fashion accessories, and then don't care for them.

These tweets will help your marketing in the long term, because they attract people who are interested in the subject matter.

6. Ask Questions

When you post questions, you'll probably get answers, which is a good thing on Twitter. It's called 'engagement', and the more engaged your followers are, the better.

Invite opinions, request advice. People enjoy giving advice, because they can be helpful without spending much time.

Any topic will do, but the most useful questions are those relating to your books' topics.

Ask a few questions, and when you receive an answer, reply.

Has anyone made bread with fresh tomatoes? Does it work? Any tips, recipes, advice?

I want to watch a vampire movie. A scary one. Recommendations?

What's your favourite vampire novel, ever?

Has anyone read 'The Vampyre' (early vampire novella by John Polidori)? Worth reading?

Let The Right One In – I love the novel. Is the film worth watching? #vampire

I'm thinking of adopting another #dog from the shelter.

7. Tweet Interesting Websites

Find breaking news, interesting blog posts or informative pages related to your books' topic. Tweet the URL, with a brief explanation of what it is about.

Archaeologists discover vampire grave. http://www.....
This is a cool site with pics of all actors who played vampires. http://www....
Fabulous vampire paintings here. Really creative. http://www....
Cute Puppy Contest. Best photo wins cash prize. http://www...
Ten Dog Training Secrets. http://www...

Twitter will show only part of the URL, so it will fit into the tweet. You can also use a URL-shortening service (see Chapter 23).

8. Quotes

Post witty, insightful or thought-provoking quotes by famous people.

I recommend this site which contains thousands of quotes, searchable by topic. http://www.brainyquote.com

Choose quotes that are related to the books you want to promote, e.g. if you write paranormal romance, pick quotes about love, romance, courtship, werewolves, vampires and such. This will attract future readers.

For Suzie Scrybe who writes vampire romances, this might be a suitable quote to tweet:

"When other little girls wanted to be ballet dancers, I kind of wanted to be a vampire." ~ Angelina Jolie

Franco Folly who writes dog training guides might tweet:

"It's not the size of the dog in the fight, it's the size of the fight in the dog." ~ Mark Twain

9. Promote Your Book

Tweet something about your book, with a URL to a site where people can buy it. These are the least popular tweets, so use them sparingly. In Chapter 17 I'll show you some techniques on how to promote your book without annoying your followers.

For now, here are some examples:

Special offer today: 'The Vamp Vanishes' by Suzie Scrybe. 99c for Kindle http...
Do you like vampires? 'The Vamp Vanishes'. Paranormal Romance. Ebook or paperback. http:...
Train Your Dog At Home – The Buddhist Way. Ebook with step-by-step instructions. http:...

WHAT NOT TO DO

Don't tweet in the heat of roused emotions (you might regret your outburst), reveal personal details (children's school schedule, credit card number), or show great vulnerability (trolls trawl Twitter in search of victims to bully).

Also, don't churn out one promotional tweet after another. People will ignore and/or unfollow you.

Don't space out tweets like this:

Do you
want to read
a great
vampire romance?
Try
The Vamp Vanishes
by
Suzie Scrybe

Hogging space in other people's timelines is inconsiderate, and it raises your followers' hackles. The only time line breaks are appreciated is for mini poems.

You don't need to read all tweets you receive. That would lead to insanity – listening to thousands of people at once! Later in the book we'll look at ways to manage the streams of tweets that arrive in your timeline.

ADVANCED STRATEGIES

Mix it up. Alternate between different kinds of tweets. There's no definite recipe, although some self-appointed gurus try to impose their rules ('40% news, 40% discussions, 10% quotes, 10% promo'). The more you mix it up, the better, especially if you add conversations and images to the blend (more about those in Chapters 7 and 8).

Go easy on the promotional tweets. Those won't attract followers; indeed, they may put people off.

Think in terms of keywords. What kind of words might the prospective readers of your books search for? Use those liberally. Suzie might use *vampire, vampires, blood, fangs, paranormal, Twilight, undead.* Franco might use *dog, dogs, puppy, puppies, obedience, training, grooming, terrier, collie, sheepdog.* Insert those frequently. You can use them with hashtags. (More about hashtags in Chapter 6.)

If you write fiction, include the name of your genre (Horror, Paranormal Romance, Steampunk, Epic Fantasy) as often as possible.

CHAPTER 3: RETWEETING

When you like someone's tweet, and want to send it to all your followers, click 'retweet'.

THE BASICS

The original tweeters will be delighted, and will often return the favour by retweeting one of yours. This is a quick way to gain the goodwill of other people, promote yourself, and keep your own followers entertained.

Retweet a few tweets for friends and fellow authors, especially those writing in the same genre. It's also worth retweeting tweets related to the topic of your books. For example, vampire romance author Suzie Scrybe could retweet interesting tweets about vampires.

However, don't overdo it. Continuous retweets, without tweets of your own, get boring. Then people will either block your retweets or unfollow you altogether.

Be careful what you retweet. Choose only tweets your followers will be interested in. Definitely read the tweets before you retweet them. If the tweets contain URLS, you may want to take a quick look if they're genuine, so you don't inadvertently spread malware.

You can ask your followers to retweet a tweet for you. Simply add *Please retweet* or *Pls RT* to your tweet. Many will oblige.

Example:
Today's the last day to get my vampire romance novel 'The Vamp Vanishes' free. (Please retweet)

However, use these requests sparingly, maybe once a month. Otherwise you come across as presumptuous.

Thanking everyone for retweeting is not necessary. It may seem the polite thing to do, but when you get hundreds of retweets a day, you would end up posting hundreds of tweets, *Thanks for the retweet,* which would be tedious for your followers. Also, most RTs are automatic, so you would be thanking robots.

If you appreciate someone's RT, consider retweeting something of theirs instead. That's a nice gesture. However, you're not obliged to do this, and it's not practical if you get many RTs.

WHAT NOT TO DO

Don't retweet any tweet without reading it, even if that person is a friend or another writer. Certain writers online post messages with hashtags including #muslimscum and #niggerswine, inciting religious and racial hatred. Do you really want to be seen endorsing this? Retweeting the wrong kind of tweet can harm your reputation.

Avoid retweeting a mass of promos for other people. Promo tweets are considered a boring nuisance on Twitter. Your aim should be to educate and entertain your followers, rather than irritate and bore them. Limit yourself to helping a friend or writer colleague now and then with a retweet of an important promo, but don't annoy your followers with five hundred promo retweets per day.

Don't get lured into review cartels. These are formal or informal agreements between people to retweet one another's tweets. It may seem a good idea – but you'd end up retweeting hundreds of tweets, most of them boring promo stuff. This would annoy your followers and they would stop paying attention.

Stay away from any app that does the retweeting for you. They are notorious nuisances, much hated by genuine Twitter users. They'll retweet a certain number of tweets by certain people each day, or they'll retweet something every time someone has retweeted one of yours. It may seem a time saver – but it's a sure way to put your followers off. The result is a stream of dull annoying promos, and you may also unwittingly spread offending messages and tweets promoting racial hatred and abuse.

ADVANCED STRATEGIES

In the long term, the best strategy is to retweet tweets your followers find interesting. Use Twitter's search for keywords related to your novel's topic. Suzie Scrybe may search for tweets containing 'vampire', Franco Folly may search for 'dogs'. Choose the most interesting ones and retweet those.

This will keep your followers entertained and hooked on your tweets. At the same time, it will network you with other people who are engaged in the same topic.

You may want to create a Twitter list (see Chapter 11) or a Tweetdeck column (see Chapter 25) of people whose tweets are worth retweeting.

When people you follow fill your timeline with endless retweets of boring promos, you don't need to unfollow them altogether. Simply go to their profile, click the cogwheel icon, scroll down and click on 'Turn off Retweets'. Problem solved. I do this with everyone who uses an automated retweeting service.

You can use another method for retweeting. This shows the tweet preceded by the original tweeter's name and 'RT', but you appear as the sender.

@SuzieScrybe tweets: *What would you do if you met a real life #vampire?*
@FrancoFolly retweets: *RT @SuzieScrybe What would you do if you met a real life vampire?*

To do this, either hit 'reply' and put 'RT' before the message, or use an app such as TweetDeck to create the retweet. It works only if the tweet is short enough to accommodate the 'RT' and the user name. Some people prefer this method, because they like being the sender of as many tweets as possible, which can help with SEO and such. However, it can also make you look self-obsessed. In my opinion, it doesn't matter much either way. Choose whatever method suits you.

If you change a tweet (either by hitting 'reply' and copy and pasting part of its contents, or by using an app), preface it with 'MRT' or 'MT' for 'modified retweet'.

@SuzieScrybe tweets: *What would you do if you met a real life #vampire?*
@FrancoFolly retweets: *MRT @SuzieScrybe "What would you do if you met a real life vampire?" Get out the garlic, lol.*

MISTAKES I MADE AND LEARNT FROM

Retweeting is the area where I made the most mistakes. Several times I thought I had hit on a clever strategy, only to find that it caused more harm than help.

When I was new on Twitter, I returned every RT favour. As I gained more followers and the number of retweets grew, I spent over an hour every day retweeting. Eventually, I realised that this was eating up my writing time, so I stopped doing it.

After a few months on Twitter, I discovered that certain people were retweeting one another's tweets, and that by joining, I could get each of my tweet retweeted a dozen times or more. Eagerly, I retweeted and retweeted. Retweet measuring apps showed that I was one of the most successfully retweeted participants in the whole Twitterverse. It seemed a fantastic strategy – until I stepped back and considered how much attention my tweets actually received. These mass retweets were sent to many people – but nobody was reading them. What's the point of a tweet getting automatically retweeted over and over, if nobody reads it?

For a short time, I used auto-retweeting apps (the notorious TweetAdder and RoundTeam). It seemed a good idea to keep the retweet loops going without spending my precious time. Soon I realised that this was a very bad thing. By automatically returning retweet favours, I inundated my followers with crappy stuff they didn't want to read. People who had loved reading my tweets and retweets now hated them. When I saw just how much harm the use of these apps was doing, I apologised to my followers, and vowed not to do it again.

For a while, I retweeted all tweets in my chats, because I felt that real tweeps deserved encouragement. But I quickly ran out of my daily allocation of tweets (see Chapter 24).

My current strategy is to be picky about what I retweet. Out of respect for my followers, I retweet only what I think is of interest to them. This includes very few promos. I no longer participate in review cartels, and I avoid retweeting automated tweets. When I retweet, it's genuine tweets by genuine people, not auto-generated tweets by bot accounts. With this new strategy, I get fewer retweets – but those are read by more people.

When someone I follow uses RoundTeam, I turn their retweets off.

CHAPTER 4: FOLLOWING AND UNFOLLOWING

People who follow you receive your tweets, and you get the tweets from the people whom you choose to follow.

THE BASICS

It's good to have many followers, especially if you want to gain exposure and spread the word about your books. But the number of followers is less important than the kind of followers.

"The quantity of your followers matters little.
The quality matters a lot."
- Rayne Hall

Ideally, you want followers who are real people (not automated accounts) who read your tweets (at least sometimes) and interact with you (when you both choose to). The ideal follower is someone who is interested in the subjects you tweet about. They may be fellow writers with whom you can talk shop, fans who've read your books and are excited to connect with the author, bookworms addicted to your genre, and people who like vampires (or puppies, mountaineering, or daffodils) as much as you do.

On Twitter you don't get to choose your followers. They choose you. You can encourage the right sort of followers by posting the kind of tweets they'll enjoy, but the decision is theirs.

If people of the less desirable kind (spam bots, porn peddlers, and people who randomly follow anyone without ever reading tweets) follow you, let them. There's no harm in them receiving your tweets. But don't follow them back.

You have control over who you follow, and here you need to have a strategy. Don't just follow anyone. Read people's profile text to decide. Follow people who have something in common with you (other writers), who share your interests (a passion for puppies, vampires or daffodils), who are potential readers (bookworms, lovers of your genre) or who are useful for your writing career (editors, agents).

Many of the people you follow will follow you back. This is how you build a quality following.

How do you find people to follow? First, spread the word. Tell the members of your online writers' group and other relevant communities that you're on Twitter, and suggest you follow one another.

Next, use Twitter's search function. Suzie Scrybe writes vampire fiction, so it's important for her to connect with people who are interested in vampires. She searches for profiles containing the words 'vampire' or 'vampires', and follows these people. Franco Folly writes about dog training, so he'll look for profiles with 'dogs', 'puppy' and the like.

Also look at who is following you. If their profiles show a shared interest, follow them back. Don't bother following people who have nothing in common with you. They probably used an automated service to follow lots of people at random, and will unfollow you soon anyway.

If you've followed someone and then find you don't like them, simply click 'unfollow', and you will no longer receive their tweets. Don't agonise over the decision; just do it. You have the right to choose. If someone seriously annoys you, click 'block'; then they won't be able to follow you.

Don't get upset if people unfollow you. This happens all the time. Several people unfollow me every day. Some of these simply don't like my tweets (tastes differ) and others are automated accounts, programmed to follow a lot of people and unfollow them soon after. They are no loss. If you want a laugh, read Chapter 34 about weird reasons why people unfollowed me on Twitter.

WHAT NOT TO DO

Don't follow everyone who follows you – many of them are automated accounts and spam bots.

Avoid apps and services that do your following for you. Choosing whom to follow is crucial. Your future success on Twitter depends on it, so don't give away that power. Auto-follow and auto-followback are against Twitter's new rules anyway.

Don't participate in any of the follow cartels of the #teamfollowback type. There are hundreds of them. By retweeting their tweets, you'll get a lot of followers – but these are followers who are not interested in your tweets; they only want you to follow them to boost their numbers. Instead, you'll annoy your genuine followers who'll soon get fed up with your constant junk tweets.

Don't buy followers. Many scammers do thriving business selling followers (*Get 20,000 followers for $20 today!!!*) Genuine followers can't be purchased. These are fake accounts, generated by the thousand.

Buying fake followers has no benefit whatsoever. It feeds people's vanity, that's all. Some people like the feeling of being popular like a celebrity – even though they know it's fake popularity, and everyone else knows it too. When you suddenly have a lot more followers than you're following, you'll look like an idiot.

It's against Twitter's rules, too. Twitter is good at spotting those mass-generated fake accounts and deletes them rapidly, so the people who spent money don't have much time to bask in their celebrity illusion anyway.

Some scammers sell 'real' followers – which means that they're selling you! They ask for your password so they can take over your account. For every 1,000 followers they give you, they follow 1,000 other people, and they charge them like they charge you. You end up following a lot of tweeps whose tweets bore or offend you. Your new followers have no interest in you either, so it's pointless. Worse: while the scammers have your password, they can use your account to send advertising messages for other companies (for which they get paid), to spread virus-laden malware, to access your personal information so they can hack your bank account, and more. Stay well clear.

ADVANCED STRATEGIES

Your best long-term strategy is to follow people who are potential readers of your books. Find people who enjoy reading, who like your genre, and have an interest in the topics you write about. Many of them will follow you back. This creates a quality 'platform' which will help you build a reputation and boost sales.

To create the best impression, aim for a balance between followings and followers, ideally with slightly more followers than you're following.

If your followers and followings are exactly the same number, it suggests that you're uncritical and following everyone back, which means it's probably an automated account and not interesting.

If you follow far more people than follow you, it means you're unpopular and even desperate, and your tweets aren't worth reading. (This applies only to larger accounts, not to small ones and newbies. While you're new to Twitter, you'll probably follow more people than are following you. That's natural. But after a while, you'll attract more and more followers, and if you're selective about who you follow back, you'll have more followers.)

If you have a lot more followers than you're following, it means you're either a genuine celebrity or (more likely) a vain fool who has purchased fake followers.

Chapter 5 contains strategies for getting more followers.

MISTAKES I MADE AND LEARNT FROM

When I was new to Twitter and eager to get followers, I participated in #teamfollowback, #instantfollowback, #autofollow and the like. This gave me a lot of followers who weren't interested in me, my books or my tweets. It filled my timeline with junk tweets, and it inundated my genuine followers with retweeted junk. After a few weeks, I realised how silly this was and stopped.

CHAPTER 5: GETTING MORE FOLLOWERS

On Twitter, having many followers is good – but only if these are real people, who are interested in your topics and read your tweets at least sometimes.

Getting lots of junk followers is easy. Quality is what counts.

THE BASICS

Aim to get as many genuine followers as you can. These will be your 'platform' - potential readers, reviewers and supporters.

The more active you are on Twitter, the more people (and automated accounts) will follow you.

Getting the first 10,000 or so followers is the most difficult. Once you have a large number of followers – like I have – you can just sit back and watch your follower numbers rise.

Here are the three main strategies for attracting many followers of the right sort:

1. Craft your profile text with care, so people with an interest in your topic find you when they search the crucial keywords. (See Chapter 1.)

2. Follow many people. A large number of them will follow you back. By choosing whom to follow, you're indirectly choosing what kind of people will follow you, so pick people who share your interests and who enjoy reading the type of books you write. Time spent on following people is a good investment.

3. Chat. Reply to people's tweets, ask them questions, engage in conversations. More about this in Chapter 8. By chatting, you show that you're a real person, not an automated account. This makes you attractive.

WHAT NOT TO DO

Stay away from any app or service that automatically follows people for you. You'd be giving away your most important power.

Don't bother following celebrities. If someone is famous, or has many times more followers than they follow, they won't be interested in following you.

If you follow too many people too quickly, Twitter will think you're a robot, and stop you. When this happens, don't panic. You just need to wait a day, and you can follow people again. More about limits in Chapter 24.

There's no need to tell people that you're following them (Twitter notifies them in the 'Connections' tab), or to thank them. Your natural courtesy may impel you to say 'thank you' but it's unnecessary and may even be annoying. Some people get Notifications on their mobile phone every time someone sends them a personal tweet by DM; their phone keeps beeping from all the 'thanks for following' tweets.

Worse: most 'thanks for following' tweets are automated, sent not by people but by apps faking a personal touch. By thanking, you'll appear to be one of those fakers.

It's not a big deal – thanking people for following you doesn't cause harm, it's just pointless. But you can spend this time more productively by reading your new followers' tweets and responding to them.

Don't use one of those annoying apps that automatically send out 'thanks for following me' tweets.

Automated messages like, *Thanks for following me. You've made my day*, show a level of insincerity that undermines your followers' trust from the start.

When you get DM tweets (and you're bound to get a lot of them) assuring you that you have made some person's day, that they are delighted to connect with you, that they look forward to reading your tweets, ignore them. These are apps programmed to say the same thing non-stop.

Don't push your book (blog, newsletter, Kickstarter, other social media) on new followers. This would make a bad first impression, and may get you instantly unfollowed.

Here are some typical examples of what not to do:
Thanks for following me. You made my day! Buy my book here: http...
Thanks for following. Please help me win the contest by voting for me http...
Great to connect! You can fund my project with Kickstarter. Http...
Thanks for following. Let's also connect at Facebook http... and Google+ http...
Thanks for following. Visit my blog http.....

ADVANCED STRATEGIES

1. Listen to 'shoutouts' in which people recommend who is worth following. These recommended people are almost always genuine.

Search for the keyword '#ff' which stands for 'Follow Friday'. Twitter will show you many tweets with lists of recommendations. However, don't follow everyone in these lists. Many won't be relevant to your interest area.

Another good shoutout hashtag is '#ww'. This stands for 'Writer Wednesday'. Every Wednesday, writers recommend other writers worth following. This is a way to connect with colleagues in your field. Beware, though - '#ww' also stands for 'Wine Wednesday' and 'Wedding Wednesday'.

2. Use other people's themed lists. Many people compile lists of tweeps – for example 'Writers', 'Romance Readers', 'Zombie Aficionados', and share them with the Twitterverse. Find lists with themes that are relevant, and follow everyone on these lists. A large number will follow you back.

Here is a list you may want to try to start with: 'Writers Follow Writers'. I've compiled a list of writers who promise to followback anyone whose profile says they're a writer/author/novelist/journalist/poet. This will quickly give you seventy or more quality followers. https://twitter.com/RayneHall/lists/writers-follow-writers.

Whenever someone puts you on a list, Twitter will notify you. Chances are, the other people on this list are exactly the kind of people you want to connect with. This is my number one successful method for gaining followers. More about lists in Chapter 11.

3. Use apps. Several apps (services) are available to help you follow people, such as Tweepi and ManageFlitter. The basic version is usually free. Use them to select who to follow. For example, you can view everyone who has the word 'vampire' in their profile text, and see at a glance how active they are, how many followers they have, and other information. This helps you choose the right people to connect with.

However, don't let the apps do the choosing for you. Stay away from any app that offers to automatically follow everyone with a certain word in their profile text.

4. This is a weird phenomenon. Many of my followers tell me that whenever they engage in a chat with me, they suddenly get new followers. I'm hesitant to mention it, because it may seem I'm boasting or touting for chats, but apparently it really works.

I think it's because chatting with anyone shows you're a real person. It's also because of how I conduct my chats so all my followers can read them (see Chapter 8), and because I have many followers. This creates a lot of exposure.

If you want to try it, go ahead (I'm @RayneHall) but please don't be angry if I don't have time to chat with you. I have books to write.

5. Unfollow the people who don't follow you back. (More about that in Chapter 24.)

MISTAKES I MADE AND LEARNT FROM

Confession: in my first year on Twitter, I bought followers. If I remember correctly, the going rate at the time was $12 for 1000. To my disgust, these 'followers' were obvious fakes: Many had near-identical profile texts, others had no profile texts at all. The same spelling errors recurred in many of the profile texts. A large number had no avatar, while a hundred others showed the same woman in different poses. What an embarrassment! I hoped nobody would see these. However, Twitter deleted most of them within three weeks anyway. This was a frustration (I had wasted my money) as well as a relief (the evidence of my stupidity was removed). Soon after, the number of genuine followers increased, and I wondered why I had bothered buying followers in the first place.

CHAPTER 6: HASHTAGS

Hashtags are not necessary – but they are extremely useful.

THE BASICS

Hashtags emphasise important words in tweets. This draws attention to those words, and makes them more searchable.

Hashtags also help like-minded people to link up. Importantly, they help readers connect with authors.

Place a hashtag (#) before the word you want to emphasise, like this: #hashtag.

You can have several hashtags in each tweet, but don't overdo it. Tweets with one or two hashtags draw attention; tweets with more than two get largely ignored.

Choose your hashtags carefully. The best hashtags not only emphasise the topic of the tweet, but the essence of your topic on Twitter, the stuff you tweet about and want to be known for.

Suzie Scrybe, vampire romance author, should try to hashtag the following words in her tweets: #vampire, #vampires, #romance, #love, #novel, #blood, #reading, #book, #paranormal.

For Franco Folly, author of a book on Zen-style dog training, useful hashtags might be: #dog, #dogs, #puppy, #puppies, #obedience, #training, #buddhism, #zen, #animals, #pets.

A hashtag emphasises only the one word immediately after it. It's okay and customary to combine several words in one hashtag: #dogtraining, #epicfantasy, #amwriting, #writetip.

It doesn't matter if you use capitals or not: '#dogtraining' and '#DogTraining' are treated as the same, although the latter may be easier to read.

HASHTAGS FOR WRITERS

Certain hashtags are used a lot by writers. Search for tweets containing those hashtags, and use them yourself:

#amwriting = here you talk about your work in progress. Good for connecting with other writers.
Example:
Have completed another chapter of my WiP #thriller. Four more to go. #amwriting

#amediting = similar to #amwriting, but about the revision process, of interest only to other writers.
Example:
I need to make the climax scene more exciting. Maybe different PoV? #amediting

#writetip (also #writingtip) = share advice with other writers
Example:
#writetip Words overused by novice writers: look, turn, start, begin, could, smile, feel, slowly, suddenly

#indiepub = for self-publishing authors, or about self-published books

#indiepubtip = advice for self-publishing authors

#NaNoWriMo = mutual support for participants of National Novel Writing Month

#writechat = writers discuss writing-related matters

#writing = anything to do with your craft

WHAT NOT TO DO

Avoid hashtags that smack of advertising. Tweets with hashtags like #unmissable, #bargain, #greatbook, #mustread, #mustbuy get ignored.

Don't load your tweets with hashtags. More than two, and your followers' eyes will glide over the tweet without reading it. Suzie Scrybe will get little attention if she tweets *#New #vampire #romance #novel #paranormal #mustread #unputdownable #greatread #mustbuy #99c for #Kindle.* I call this #hashtag #diarrhoea.

Stephen King says: "The #road to #hell is #paved with #hashtags."

HASHTAG BLINDNESS

Some Twitter users have grown to ignore all hashtags. Their eyes skim over the hashtagged words, and this can lead to misunderstandings. For a while, Nat Russo (@NatRusso) posted a series of tongue-in-cheek tweets for writers, using the hashtag #HorribleWriteTip. Example: *For maximum effect, make sure all of your sentences contain the same number of syllables. #HorribleWriteTip*

Surprisingly many people ignored the hashtag, thought he was serious, and attacked him for giving such advice.

Perhaps he could have avoided the misunderstanding by adding ';-)' or 'LOL' to the tweets. But the point is, people ignored the hashtag. Instead of standing out, it faded out of people's awareness. Such 'hashtag blindness' might occur in your followers, too, so don't rely on the hashtagged word to carry the meaning.

ADVANCED STRATEGIES

Use your genre as a hashtag: #horror, #epicfantasy, #paranormal. This brings readers of your genre to you – the ideal audience.

What are the key hashtags used by fans of your genre? Use them frequently in your tweets.

Hashtag non-promotional tweets as well as promos.

Use hashtags already in use by other people. This will increase their popularity and success.

Use hashtags which are currently trending, perhaps connected to current affairs. Can you tweet about whatever is in the news, in a way that's relevant to your genre? If yes, this is an opportunity for hashtagging and attracting attention.

If you're ambitious, create a hashtag for your book's title: #StormDancer, #ThirtyScaryTales, #WritingFightScenes. This is unlikely to lead to success because few people search for these terms. However, sometimes it works. Twice, I managed to make #StormDancer a worldwide trending hashtag, a success most marketing gurus dream of.

You can also have hashtag fun by linking words together for emphasis, especially in a joking way.

Procrastination: publisher's deadline looms, book isn't finished, haven't written a word all day. #butiwilldefinitelywritetomorrow

Yes, Sulu, I will buy you a catnip mouse on eBay. No, Sulu, I will not buy a xxxfy79, whatever that is. #getoffmykeyboard.

MISTAKES I MADE AND LEARNT FROM

I used to hashtag all my book titles in promo tweets like this: *A siege commander fights to protect women from the evil inside him. #StormDancer http://viewBook.at/B005MJFV58*

Although this does no harm, it's pointless, so I've decided to phase this out. In future, I'll use the #StormDancer hashtag only for special events, such as contests and TwitterParties (see Chapter 19).

When another publisher brought out a novel whose title was near-identical to mine, and started using my hashtag, I was angry. They were piggy-backing on my success, and it felt like theft. Now I know this is no cause for worry. Far from damaging my hashtag, they were boosting its popularity.

CHAPTER 7: ATTACHING PICTURES

Images get more attention in social media than text posts. You can make your tweets more interesting by attaching pictures.

THE BASICS

Attaching pictures on Twitter is easy - just click the camera icon at the bottom of the text box. As long as the picture is small and the tweet is short, a link appears and viewers can click that. However, tweets get much more attention if a picture is visible than if there's a link to click.

This brings us to a Great Twitter Mystery: how to make the pictures visible. Often, Twitter just shows a link, and at other times, just part of a picture.

I experimented extensively over the months. Whatever I tried, whatever strategies I pursued, nothing quite worked. I tried format, size, resolution, frequency, etc. It always showed for some people but not others, and there was no consistency about who saw what. If I posted three tweets with pics A, B, and C, some people saw A, some B, some C, with no discernible pattern based on settings, browser or anything.

At last, I discovered the 'magic formula': *Make the image precisely 1024 pixels wide and 512 pixels high. Do not deviate a single pixel. Set the resolution to 72 ppi. Post the picture at midnight when the moon is full.*

It still won't show for everyone, because of factors outside your control, for example, what device and app the person uses to read their tweets. But most people will see the picture.

Twitter will turn your image into an URL, and then turn it back into an image. The URL counts as part of your 140 characters, so if you attach a picture, your tweets need to be even shorter than usual.

SHOWING YOUR BOOK COVERS

The obvious pictures to tweet are of course your book covers. The more often someone sees a cover, the more inclined they are to buy the book. Don't overdo it, though. Your followers don't want to see the same book cover twenty-four times a day.

Book covers are vertical, while the ideal Twitter picture is horizontal. If you tweet the cover as it is, it'll show only in part or not at all. Paste it on a horizontal background of 1024x512 pixels. If you don't have the digital image manipulation skills, enlist the help of a Photoshop- or GIMP-savvy friend.

This my Twitter-sized image of the Storm Dancer cover:

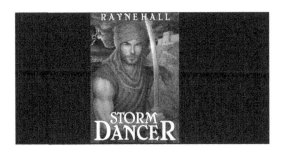

For variety, crop different parts of your cover, so you're not tweeting the same picture over and over. These are the cropped images for Storm Dancer:

You can also combine several book covers in one picture, like I did here:

OTHER PICTURES YOU CAN TWEET

Photos of cute pets are always popular, and they add a personal touch amidst all the promo tweets. Here's my cat Sulu in the birdbath:

Tweet pictures which are related to your book, but not about your book. For example, Suzie Scrybe can share pictures of vampires, and Franco Folly of dogs.

Funny images are best. A picture which raises a smile or chuckle will be favourited and retweeted many times and may go viral.

The target audience of my Writer's Craft books are writers, and so are many of my followers. Therefore, I tweet pictures about writing. I have tweeted many pithy comments about the writer's craft, and hit on the idea of illustrating them. Since I can't paint, I hired cartoonists. Here are some of the results. My followers love them. The blonde bespectacled woman is me.

Book lovers are my target audience, too, so I commissioned some pictures about reading, too.

My followers enjoy the cartoons of Merlin The Book-Loving Cat especially. They raise smiles because people like cats and often recognise their own felines' behaviour. Each picture features one of my books – but in an unobtrusive way. The pictures are about Merlin; the books are just props. This creates exposure for my books without annoying my followers.

Here are some examples of Merlin promoting *Storm Dancer* and *Thirty Scary Tales:*

Could you adapt this idea for your own books? Don't copy it slavishly, but use it as inspiration. What kind of recurring character could you use to interact with your books, or to represent them? Franco Folly's images could feature a cute puppy, while funny vampire cartoons would captivate Suzie Scrybe's audience.

WHERE TO FIND PICTURES

Create your own, if you have artistic skills. Draw, sketch, sculpt, paint and photograph.

Invite creative friends and family members to contribute.

Ask your children to paint vampire pictures for you as gifts on birthdays, Christmas and other occasions. It solves their problem what to give Mum this year. Children's pictures rouse smiles. You can tweet:

This is my 8-year-old's idea of a #vampire.
My niece (age 10) has painted this picture of a #puppy for my birthday. Isn't it cute?

Find beautiful art online, download it, then attach it to the tweet – but only if you have the artist's permission, and with the artist's name in the tweet. A great site to find art is DeviantArt.com. You need to join (it's free); then you can contact the artists. Some won't reply, others will decline. But many will be delighted by the free exposure and promotion. You can tweet:

This painting of #vampire love by [Artist Name] is awesome.

I've just found this painting of a #vampire. He looks just like [Hero's Name] in [Novel Title].

These #puppies are the cutest thing ever. Photographed by [photographer's name].

When your followers respond and discuss the pictures, you can guide them to the artist's DeviantArt page or website.

Commission an artist. You can hire an artist to create images just for you. Prices for this vary greatly. I started by commissioning seven pictures, then ten more, then twenty... gradually building a collection of 150 cartoons. Several artists contributed, but most are by @DoNichiArt. Most days, I tweet one or two cartoons, and when I've posted them all, I start over. I also use them on Facebook, Google+, YouTube, Pinterest and other social networks, and to illustrate blog posts. These cartoons gain me far more attention and goodwill than paid advertisements, and are cheaper, too.

WHAT NOT TO DO

Continuous promo tweets with pictures of your book cover make your Twitter offerings look like an advertising channel.

ADVANCED STRATEGIES

If you create your own images or hire someone to create them for you, aim for consistency. Use recurring elements, for example, the same character (I used the blonde bespectacled writer and the grey cat), the same shape and colours (I use blue squares with turquoise frames).

Make sure your name appears in the picture. This doesn't apply to images you've borrowed, but if you create or commission your own, then you should reap the full benefits. If a picture goes viral, you want your name connected to it. The writer's craft memes include my name beneath the quote, and the cat cartoons show my name discreetly on the books.

Consider making the images part of your visual branding strategy by using the same colour scheme as for your book covers, business card and website. For example, if your book covers are pink and purple, create pink and purple cartoons. This helps your audience to mentally connect the cartoons with your books.

If you make or commission images, use them in other social media as well.

MISTAKES I MADE AND LEARNT FROM

I commissioned the first cartoons before I discovered the 'magic formula' of making images visible in the timeline. By the time I realised that a horizontal format was ideal, the blue squares were already popular, so I continued them (but presented them on a horizontal background).

CHAPTER 8: CONVERSATIONS

Chats with like-minded people are the lifeblood of all social media. They're the 'social' part, and they count. Unfortunately, many writers use Twitter as a dumping site for their promotions, wasting a great opportunity.

THE BASICS

Time spent chatting with other people on Twitter is one of the best investments you can make in your publishing business. It's free, it's fun, and it's super-effective.

When you chat, you show that you're a real person, not an automated account. Amidst all the auto-tweets, promo-dumps and fakes, you will stand out. People will become interested in you. Many will follow you simply because you're real! This way, your platform will grow rapidly.

When you chat with people, they become curious about you. They'll read your profile, see that you're an author, maybe click through to your website or bookselling link. If the book appeals, they'll read the description, maybe download the sample chapter, and this often leads to sales.
Don't expect everyone you chat with to buy your book – but it happens frequently. Often it's not the person you chatted with, but eavesdroppers who become customers this way.

To start a chat, simply pick a tweet someone sent, that you find interesting, maybe by viewing random tweets in your timeline. Hit 'reply' and write a comment, or better still, a question. People will be delighted that you've noticed their tweet and that you're taking an interest.

Twitter will show the user name of the other person at the beginning of the tweet. Only people who follow both of you can read your exchange.

Here's an example of a conversation. On the day I wrote this chapter, Wiebke (@hab318princess) and I (@RayneHall) chatted:

hab318princess tweets: *looking forward to the weekend... need to find discipline to actually keep writing #procrastination*
RayneHall tweets: *@hab318princess What are you #writing?*
hab318princess tweets: *m/m novel with original characters (I started out in fanfiction)*
RayneHall tweets: *@hab318princess Is this your first original #fiction project?*
hab318princess tweets: *@RayneHall No, I have done Nanowrimo before*
RayneHall tweets: *@hab318princess I've never tried #writing #fanfiction. I enjoy creating my own worlds.*
hab318princess tweets: *@RayneHall I took part in a school writing course at 13 - all based on prompts - fanfiction was an easy way into writing 20+ years later*
RayneHall tweets: *@hab318princess m/m - is that gay romance? I imagine that's a challenging genre for a female #author to write. Why did you pick it? #curious*

hab318princess tweets: *yes, it is gay romance. I started writing in the #Torchwood fandom and the main couple was Jack/Ianto... it went from there 1/2*
hab318princess writes: *@RayneHall 2/2 research helps as well as reading in the genre (the internet is a mine of information)*

Other people may jump into the conversation. That's useful and fun. Go for it. The drawback is that the list of user names in the reply tweets gets longer and longer, leaving little room for the actual post. Then conversations look like this:

SuzieScrybe tweets: *@book-thrills @FrancoFolly @mark_cassell @douglaskolacki @kevinomclaughlin @aprilgreynyc @taramayastales @jb121jonathan @RayneHall Do you?*
book_thrills tweets: *@SuzieScrybe @FrancoFolly @mark_cassell @douglaskolacki @kevinomclaughlin @aprilgreynyc @taramayastales @jb121jonathan @RayneHall No*

This suffocates the conversation. To get around it, remove the user names of people who're no longer actively contributing to the chat.

Often, people jump into ongoing chats without reading all the preceding tweets, especially when one of those annoying auto-retweeting apps retweets a tweet without context, which can lead to misunderstandings.

Typical Twitter chats go fast, especially if you have several people join. Typos slip in. Don't worry about those in your own tweets, and be courteous enough to overlook them in other people's.

It's fine to eavesdrop on other people's conversations. Whenever there's live chat going on, ears perk. Hundreds of people may take notice of what you say. This is a great way to gain attention and exposure.

When I share fun chats with people, I think I'll remember them forever, but with so much going on, it's easy to forget with whom I talked about what, especially if they keep changing their avatar pictures. I've started a private list (see Chapter 11) for people with whom I had enjoyable conversations, although I don't always remember to add everyone to it. Another way to preserve valued chats is to 'favourite' those tweets, so they'll be saved.

WHAT NOT TO DO

Don't post overt promos for your books, disguised as conversations. Nobody is interested in those, so you're wasting your time. Your followers are not stupid. They know that chats like this one are arranged by Suzie Scrybe:

FrancoFolly tweets: *I've just read The Vamp Vanishes by Suzie Scrybe. Awesome #vampire book. Recommended! #greatread*

Book_Thrills tweets: *I agree, The Vamp Vanishes is the best vampire in a single night, I just couldn't put it down! #mustread #vampire*
Calamity_Cass tweets: *Thanks for the recommendation. I absolutely must read The Vamp Vanishes. Where can I buy it?*

Don't hijack other people's conversations to dump your book promotions like this (fictional) prat does:

FrancoFolly tweets: *@SuzieScrybe I've finished reading the Vamp Vanishes. Great book.*
SuzieScrybe tweets: *@FrancoFolly Thanks! Which is your favourite part of it?*
FrancoFolly tweets: *The bit where the vampires steal the garlic – it's hilarious.*
StupidPrat tweets: *@FrancoFolly @SuzieScrybe My novel The Vampire Vanessa is hilarious. You must read it. You'll love it.*
SuzieScrybe tweets: *@FrancoFolly I had fun writing that garlic theft scene. Would you consider reviewing the book on Amazon?*
FrancoFolly tweets: *@SuzieScrybe Sure. I'll post a review tomorrow.*
StupidPrat tweets: *@FrancoFolly @SuzieScrybe Review my book too. I'll send it to you FREE!!!! I know you'll love it.*
SuzieScrybe writes: *@stupidprat @FrancoFolly We're talking about The Vamp Vanishes.*
StupidPrat writes: *@SuzieScrybe @FrancoFolly I know, but my book is about vampires too, and it's a #greatbook #mustread.*

ADVANCED STRATEGIES

You can write longer by using '...' at the end of a tweet and then reply to the tweet itself, or you can number your tweets (1/3, 2/3, 3/3).

To build a focused platform for your book, chat about topics relevant to your genre (for example, if you write paranormal romance, chat about vampires and werewolves), and hashtag the keywords liberally. Do this without mentioning your books, unless someone specifically asks about them.

To make your conversations visible to more people, put a full stop before the user name in your replies. It's a nifty way to invite eavesdroppers and gain attention – if this is what you want. Here's an example of a real conversation. Note how several of us are using the full stop trick.

Mark_Cassell tweets: *Five... Days... Off! :-D*
RayneHall tweets: *.@Mark_Cassell Five days off what?*
Mark_Cassell tweets: *.@RayneHall Hmm, very true... Five days off the day job. But not writing! I have a Steampunk story to finish for you. Don't worry.*
RayneHall tweets: *.@Mark_Cassell I look forward to reading it. I may (or may not) accept it for Cogwheels: Ten Tales of Steampunk.*
Mark_Cassell tweets: *.@RayneHall Fingers crossed you'll like it! It was fun to write. I had to read some #Steampunk first, and also research the genre itself.*
RayneHall tweets: *.@Mark_Cassell I like your fiction. Nicely dark and scary:-D so I look forward to this one. Does it straddle #steampunk and #horror?*

Mark_Cassell tweets: .*@RayneHall It certainly crosses genres. I've always written #horror, so just had to throw a few cogs into the mix... and other stuff.*

RayneHall tweets: .*@Mark_Cassell I've accepted some fine #steampunk stories for this anthology already, by @Aprilgreynyc, @BethDaniels1 and others.*

Mark_Cassell tweets: .*@RayneHall Hmm, there's some tough competition with @Aprilgreynyc & @BethDaniels1. I'll be sure to polish every brass edge! :-D*

RayneHall tweets.*@Mark_Cassell Your writing style & approach to storytelling is very different from theirs. I like the variety @Aprilgreynyc @BethDaniels1*

Mark_Cassell tweets: .*@RayneHall Variety is important in anthologies. It would be dull if all the stories were in a similar style. @Aprilgreynyc @BethDaniels1*

Aprilgreynyc tweets: *@Mark_Cassell @RayneHall @BethDaniels1 #steampunk I look forward to Cogs. Hope my story is still in.*

RayneHall tweets: .*@Aprilgreynyc Your story is definitely in :-) It was the first story I accepted for this anthology. @Mark_Cassell @BethDaniels1*

@Mark_Cassell tweets: .*@RayneHall Variety is important in anthologies. It would be dull if all the stories were in a similar style. @Aprilgreynyc @BethDaniels1*

Rayne Hall tweets: .*@Mark_Cassell Variety is why readers love anthologies. Stories on the same topic by diff authors in diff styles @Aprilgreynyc @BethDaniels1*

BthDaniels1 tweets: *@Aprilgreynyc @RayneHall @Mark_Cassell Variety is good! :-)*

RayneHall tweets: .*@BethDaniels1 Yes. Readers who review the Ten Tales anthos often praise the variety @Aprilgreynyc @Mark_Cassell*

Aprilgreynyc tweets: .*@Mark_Cassell @RayneHall @BethDaniels1 my favorite steampunk novel was The glass books of the Dream Eaters! Actually sev. Volumes.*
Mark_Cassell tweets: *.@Aprilgreynyc Seven volumes? That's a lot. Did it grip you all the way along? @RayneHall @BethDaniels1*
Aprilgreynyc tweets: *@Mark_Cassell @RayneHall @BethDaniels1 LOL. That's the typo! 3 volumes but they split vol. 1 into two so like a tetrology. I was addicted!*
Mark_Cassell tweets: *@Aprilgreynyc Ha! Don't you love typos! :-D. If they're that good, I'll go get them. Addiction can be okay... @RayneHall @BethDaniels1*

Alternatively, type the message before the user name. I used to do this, shifting names to the end - but then eavesdroppers didn't realise these were replies. They saw the messages out of context, misunderstood their meaning, and responded as if I had made a general statement.

You may want to read a conversation thread before you add to it. However, Twitter doesn't make this easy. You need to click 'view conversation' to see the past few tweets of the chat, repeat this until you get to the start, and even then, you'll get to see only the main thread.

If you're involved in a conversation, it's best to focus on it. Read the incoming tweets in the Notifications tab (also called 'Interactions' or 'Connect').

MISTAKES I MADE AND LEARNT FROM

My main problem with chats is that I get carried away and stay online much longer than I had intended. For example, I wanted to write three chapters, starting with this one. I logged into Twitter to quickly get some sample conversations. Those chats led to others, and I enjoyed myself so much that I forgot the time. At midnight, I remembered that I had meant to write three chapters that day.

At one stage, I decided to encourage genuine tweets by retweeting entire chats. But that overwhelmed my followers, and I soon exceeded the daily quota of tweets allowed by Twitter, so I had to stop.

CHAPTER 9: DIRECT MESSAGES

Direct Messages (DM) allow you to communicate with another person, without the whole Twitterverse listening in.

THE BASICS

DM is great if you want to exchange confidential information, for example, swap email addresses. But almost everything you receive in your DM inbox is crap – tweets sent by robots, automatic replies, spam, and a lot of links containing malware.

Hackers use DM to hijack your account by sending you an infected URL. They tweet *Haha, have you seen this photo of you?* or *This person is writing really nasty things about you* to trick you into clicking. As soon as you've clicked that link, they gain access to your password, infect your account with malware, and send infect DM tweets to all your followers.

To stay safe, don't click on any link you receive by DM, not even if it comes from your friends, because their accounts may have been hijacked by hackers.

This has been a huge problem for as long as I've been on Twitter, and staff seem unable to stop it because the offenders constantly change the wording.

Most tweets you receive by DM are promos of some kind, usually sent with one of those annoying automation apps. Even seemingly personal messages are automated. A large number come from people you've just followed, and are mostly of the presumptuous kind: *Thanks for following me. Please also like my Facebook/read my blog/buy my novel/fund my Kickstarter.*

You can ignore them all.

Another kind of nuisance DM is the demand that you validate yourself. You follow someone, and they send you an automated request to prove that you're real. Ignore them.

"Validation service users: You expect me to prove to your robot that I'm not a robot?

Go bite yourself in the buttocks."
- Rayne Hall

You can only DM people who follow you, so if you want to DM a non-follower, you need to ask them to follow you first: *Hi @SuzieScrybe, I want to send you a DM. Could you follow me, please?*

WHAT NOT TO DO

Don't promote your books via DM. This will get you unfollowed fast.

Don't send automated 'thanks for following me' DM messages. I get hundreds of those every week and they're a nuisance. If you currently use an app to send those annoying DM auto-thanks, turn them off.

ADVANCED STRATEGIES

Many people ignore the whole DM thing altogether, and never even open their DM inbox. This is a valid strategy which increases your safety and saves you time.

CHAPTER 10: DEALING WITH SPAMMERS, TROLLS AND TROUBLEMAKERS

Nuisances abound everywhere in social media. On Twitter, it's easy to shut them out.

THE BASICS

You choose from whom you want to hear. Anyone who annoys you, you can simply unfollow.

They can still send you tweets if they preface them with your user name like this: *@SuzieScrybe The stupid cow! How dare you unfollow me?!*

When that happens, click 'block'. Now they can no longer follow you, see your tweets or tweet you.

Don't hesitate to unfollow and block annoying people. It's your Twitter. You're in charge.

SPAMMERS

Some people tweet constant promos, advertising their book, product or service. Those are annoying, but are not spam. You can simply ignore them. If they get on your nerves, unfollow these people.

Spam is a particularly irritating form of promo, the kind that doesn't respect your privacy and finds way to break through the barriers you've put up. The line between 'promo' and 'spam' is thin, and there is not always a clear difference.

Basically, if you choose to follow someone, it means you give them permission to tweet about their products. These promo tweets are boring and perhaps irritating, but they're not spam. Spam is when you did not give permission, and they pester you anyway. For example, if you don't follow someone, and they throw their promos at you anyway by addressing them to your user name:
@SuzieScrybe Get rich quick! Here's the way to earn money in your spare time. URL....

Spammers also abuse DM (direct messaging) to force their unwanted promos on people.

Click on the person's profile, then on the cogwheel icon. Scroll down and click 'report for spam'.

Twitter deals harshly with such offenders, by suspending or deleting their accounts. In my experience, this happens very fast. Sometimes I report an account for spam, and within seconds, that account is suspended.

Much spam is sent from bot accounts. The spammer create thousands of accounts, and each continuously spams thousands of individuals. As soon as Twitter suspends one of them, they automatically create a replacement.

Don't waste time arguing with notorious spammers. Simply report them.

On the other hand, if the spammer is clearly new to Twitter, perhaps an indie author who naively thinks that's the way to promote her book, you may want to tell her gently that this is not how it works.

HATE-MONGERS

Some people use Twitter to attack those of different beliefs, orientations and ethnics. They post aggressive tweets with hashtags like #muslimscum and #niggerswine, and call for all gays to be shot.

Arguing with them would only give them more exposure. Simply ignore them. You may also want to unfollow them. Definitely don't retweet their tweets. Personally, I want nothing to do with these hatemongers. If anyone incites religious, political or racial hatred, I block them.

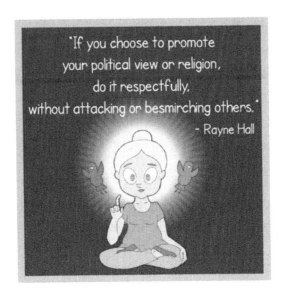

"If you choose to promote
your political view or religion,
do it respectfully,
without attacking or besmirching others."
- Rayne Hall

QUARREL-SEEKERS

Sooner or later, you'll encounter people who want to provoke you into a fight. They pick one of your tweets and argue the contents in a hostile way. They may also criticise the style and content of your tweets. They're not looking for a friendly exchange of differing opinions, or to help you to tweet better, but for an argument. Their tweets become increasingly offensive. When you tell them to stop, they'll tweet something like: *@SuzieScrybe You bitch you are trying to shut me up because you're afraid of honest discussion.*

As soon as you suspect that someone is a quarrel-seeker, discontinue the conversation. Simply ignore them. If they persist, unfollow or block them.

Don't waste your emotional energy on them. You have better things to do.

When someone tries to incite me to a fight, I may reply with one of these tweets:

If you're trying to pick a fight, find someone else. I'm not available.
or
If you don't like my tweets, simply unfollow me.
and perhaps
Do me a favour and block me, so I don't follow you again by mistake.

TROLLS AND CYBER-BULLIES

This species is similar to the quarrel-seeker, but on a larger scale. They devote their time and energy to finding and hounding victims. They're best-known under the name 'cyber-bullies' but on Twitter, the term 'troll' is more common because it's shorter.

The troll's preferred victim is someone vulnerable and emotional. If you tweet about how unhappy you are because nobody loves you, he may home in on you like a wolf.

First, he provokes you with insults or by accusing you of something you haven't done. If you respond emotionally – with anger or hurt – he's delighted and launches a full-scale attack. He'll tweet nasty things about you – for example, that you're a paedophile. Every troll has dozens (or hundreds) of Twitter accounts, and he retweets these accusations from each of them, so it feels like you're getting hounded from all sides.

Next, he uses his fake accounts to provide 'evidence' of your alleged wrongdoing. A woman claims that you raped her daughter. A retired police officer reports that he arrested you, but sadly you got away through a legal loophole. A child protection society states that you are a notorious predator and they wish you were behind bars so you could not harm more innocents.

This continues 24 hours a day, every day, and can drive you to despair. The more you protest and defend yourself, the more intense the persecution becomes.

The way to stop this is simple: Do not respond.

I know this goes against every instinct, since you want to defend your honour and stop the lies. But every response provides fuel for the troll. Trolls thrive on responses. They relish your anger and hurt. If you deprive them of this pleasure, they get bored and go in search of a more responsive victim.

If you've already responded, stop now. The troll will keep trying for a few more days, but eventually gives up. Be warned, though: he may return after a few months to have another go at you.

Resist the temptation to respond. Use 'block user' to shut trolls out of your awareness.

As this book is going to press, Twitter has finally added a feature for reporting abusive people: Go to the user's profile, click 'Block or Report', click 'This user is abusive' and fill in the form.

MISTAKES I MADE AND LEARNT FROM

In my early days on Twitter, I rose to provocations from quarrel-seekers. I explained and defended, and this wasted much of my time and caused me stress. These days, I find it easy to recognise quarrel-seekers and their strategies. I ignore hostile tweets, and if someone persists in annoying me, I have no qualms about hitting 'block'.

CHAPTER 11: LISTS

Once you follow more than a hundred or so people, it's useful to put them into lists.

THE BASICS

In real life, you interact with different kinds of people – colleagues, family, relatives, neighbours, writing buddies, college, church, club, shop staff, officials, fellow geeks. You don't interact with them all at the same time, and you wouldn't try to listen to them all at once. Instead, you meet the members of your church on Sunday mornings and the debating society on Thursday nights, you chat with your colleagues at lunch breaks and with your family when you get home from work. At major family events, you meet distant relatives, and you consult your writing buddies when you want their input in your current story.

Twitter works the same way. You can group the people you follow by subject, purpose or other criteria, and so sometimes listen to one lot, then other times another.

To create lists, go to your profile page. Click 'lists'. Click 'create new list'.

Here are some ideas for lists you could create:

* Fans
* Writing buddies
* Personal friends
* Authors you admire

* Writers who work in the same genre as you
* Readers of your genre
* People you chat with regularly
* People who tweet about a certain topic you're interested in
* Useful resources
* Potential readers of your books

Populate these lists bit by bit. Click on the person's profile, then the cogwheel icon, then 'add to list'. Then select which list (or lists) they belong to.

Whenever you visit Twitter, you can choose what kind of people you want to meet today: Do you want to interact with other writers, to listen to sage advice from experts, or to chat with your fans?
Simply click on the list of your choice, and you'll see only tweets by those people.

Lists can be 'public' or 'private'.

With public lists, you're networking and providing a service connecting like-minded people. But certain lists are best kept for your eyes only, such as 'People who pick me up when I feel low' and 'People I'm hoping to impress'.

I have 36 lists, half of them public, and I keep changing, renaming and deleting them.

Getting included in other people's lists is great, because it leads to more followers and exposure. I'm in a whopping 1,552 lists.

Whenever someone adds you to a list, Twitter notifies you in the Notification tab. Explore that list – it probably contains exactly the kind of people you want to network with.

From time to time, someone will add you to an inappropriate list. I'm on lists titled 'Wannabe Writers' and 'Fish Restaurants'. It matters little. Have a laugh and shrug it off.

USING OTHER PEOPLE'S LISTS

The lists compiled by other people are a great resource for you. Here you can read interesting tweets and find like-minded people to follow. To see useful lists, go to the profile of someone who tweets about your subject and has a large following. Click 'lists' and scroll down. Open the interesting lists, and you'll see people to follow. Then return to the person's 'lists' page, and this time click 'member of'. Here you'll discover many more useful lists.

WHAT NOT TO DO

Don't waste your time creating a list 'people who follow me' because you can see your followers by clicking 'home' and 'followers'.

Compiling a list of 'writers' is unnecessary, because hundreds of people have assembled this kind of list already. Use theirs and save your time.

Take care not to reveal confidential information about others. Keep lists like 'Depression Sufferers' and 'Adult Video Swap' private.

ADVANCED STRATEGIES

If you want to read people's tweets without following them, put them in a list. This can be useful for celebrities whose tweets you find entertaining but who won't follow you back.

Once you use TweetDeck (see Chapter 25), you can use your Twitter lists as the basis for TweetDeck columns.

If you're into SEO, create a list with your keyword, and maintain and publicise it. If the list is popular, it'll help your search engine ranking. (For most authors, SEO is not an issue though, so you can skip this step.)

MISTAKES I MADE AND LEARNT FROM

In my first year on Twitter, I created lists of genre writers ('Horror Authors', 'Fantasy Authors' and so on) and tweeted about them. This was popular – but people expected me to curate those lists, to expand them and keep them updated, and they complained when I did not. Keeping a public list updated involves a lot of work, constantly checking that accounts are still live and active, and I have other things to do. So now I have few public lists, and with the exception of 'Writers Follow Writers', 'Ten Tales Authors' and 'Procrastinating Writers Club' I don't attempt to keep them up to date.

CHAPTER 12: CREATIVE WRITING

Twitter can help you become a better writer and show off your prose skills.

THE BASICS

With a maximum of 140 characters, tweets force us to write tight. This is useful practice for writers, getting us into the habit of finding precise words and expressing ourselves concisely. There's no room for wordy waffling.

At the same time, Twitter encourages thoughtfulness and wit, and you receive instant feedback in the form of retweets and favourites.

Conversations on Twitter require even tighter writing, because each tweet has to make room for the other person's user name. This is the perfect training for writing pithy dialogue. Soon your mind becomes conditioned to firing off sizzling, zinging dialogue.

To improve your writing skills, follow hashtags such as #writetip and #writingtips, and learn from your colleagues. Some famous authors, agents and editors also post advice. This is a great resource, and it's free.

The hashtag #writingprompt provides inspiration. As you sit down to your daily writing session, search '#writingprompt' and use the first suggestion that comes up.

ADVANCED STRATEGIES

Many writers hone their craft and show off their skills with 'twitterature'. They write complete stories in a single tweet (sometimes called 'twisters'), or slightly longer ones in which every tweet covers one plot event. If you're good at this, people will follow you to read your offerings.

Round-robin writing works well on Twitter. Find several writers, take turns writing the next sentence of a story, and let the plot twists surprise you. This guarantees a lot of fun for the writers, and attracts eavesdroppers.

Twitter lends itself to very short poems. The haiku form is popular, and many writers post haiku regularly or write them on the spur of the moment as part of a conversation.

The format to follow is this: three lines, the first line containing five syllables, the second seven, the third five.

Real haiku are simple-seeming poems with deep meaning and spiritual content. On Twitter, haiku are simple and fun. Instead of spirituality, they offer humour, and instead of depth, entertainment.

CHAPTER 13: NETWORKING WITH WRITERS

Twitter is a great place to meet other writers, to hang out with them and to talk shop with colleagues. No need for introductions, group memberships or formal communities, you can connect instantly and bonds form fast.

HOW TO FIND WRITERS

Search profiles for keywords such as *writer, writing, author, novelist, debut novel, poet, journalist.*

Search tweets for hashtags: *#writing, #amwriting, #amediting, #writechat, #writingchat, #writerchat, #writingprompt.*

Check other people's themed lists (see Chapter 11).

NETWORKING

Here are some suggestions on how you can benefit from networking with other writers and publishing professionals on Twitter:

* Talk shop with like-minded people
* Ask other writers for advice about plot, writing, publishing, marketing
* Share warnings about publishing scams
* Promote one another's books and special events
* Learn from professionals (some of them post regular *#writetip* or *#writingtip* tweets)
* Provide cheerleading and moral support
* Motivate one another to writing discipline

* Share inspirational pictures and quotes
* Find critiquers and beta readers
* Eavesdrop on what publishers, editors and agents say
* Share information about contests and markets
* Share good and bad experiences with publishers etc.
* Find out which writers' groups and organisations are worth joining
* Get guidance about the submissions or indie-publishing process
* Organise joint events with other authors of the same genre
* Ask grammar questions
* Learn about publishing etiquette
* Celebrate one another's successes
* Find guest bloggers for your blog
* Get recommendations for proofreaders, editors, formatters, cover designers
* Contact authors you admire – they'll often be happy to chat, at least briefly
* Work on joint mini-writing projects (Twitterature, see Chapter 12)
and more.

Be as helpful as you can to other writers – it'll only take a few seconds to reply to a question – and don't be shy asking for assistance. Most are happy to help out with ideas, contacts, suggestions and advice.

I love networking with other writers. On Twitter, I can do this whenever I want to, spending as much or as little time as I wish.

I've asked writers for ideas what to call a steampunk telephone, or what dog breed would be most suitable for a particular story scenario, and received many suggestions.

Whenever there's a word on the tip of my tongue, I ask my Twitter followers. When I tweeted *Tip of my tongue - a saying about mutual favours, when Person A does something for Person B who does something for Person A. Can you help?* they immediately put their brains into gear on my behalf and offered possible phrases, including the one on the tip of my tongue (which was 'mutual backscratching').

If I need a discipline boost to get writing, I ask my followers to kick my butt. I promise to write a specific number of words, or to write for a certain time, and they hold me accountable. Knowing that they are awaiting my report keeps me disciplined.

It's always such a relief when other writers procrastinate as much as I do.

— Rayne Hall

As well as authors, I've found other useful professional contacts among my followers – for example, the proofreader I hired for this book is @ProofreadJulia.

When I want recommendations – a software to buy, a service to subscribe to, a book formatter to hire – I ask my Twitter followers, and listen to their suggestions and warnings.

In turn, I help Twitter followers by suggesting editors they can hire, book cover designers and illustrators who can create exactly the image they want, the best online critique groups and more.

BE HELPFUL

Find ways to help other writers. Watch out for tweets in which a writer asks for information, opinions or advice. Often, all you need to do is give a quick opinion (*I prefer the one on the right*) fact (*Both are correct in British English*) or link (*You may find this blog post helpful – http ....*).

If you don't have the answer, you can help by retweeting the question to your followers.

Having worked in publishing for three decades, edited magazines and anthologies, had my own books published by several publishers in several languages, and indie-published many books, I know a lot about the industry. I make a point of answering my followers' questions about writing and publishing. Since I have the knowledge at my fingertips, typing the answers isn't a big job. However, I do this only on Twitter, because here nobody expects more than 140 characters in reply.

When people ask me writing and publishing questions, I always reply with a full stop before the user name – like this: .user name – so all my followers benefit from my advice. Many of my followers enjoy learning from me in this 'lurking' mode.

Sometimes my answers spread over several tweets, as I answer a series of questions. Occasionally, I'll provide more detailed replies by email.

However, I draw the line when people ask me to read their novels, provide feedback on their WiPs, write a synopsis for them or review their books on Amazon.

MEETING AGENTS AND EDITORS

While I don't know to what extent other editors find writers on Twitter, I'm sure I'm not the only one.

The *Ten Tales* anthologies of fantasy and horror stories are not open for submissions, because I don't want to get inundated and have to read slush. Mostly, I select stories that have been previously published elsewhere, and sometimes I invite a writer to submit a specific kind of story.

For example, Liv Rancourt (@livrancourt) and I chatted about what makes vampires so fascinating. At the time I was editing *Bites: Ten Tales of Vampires*. She seemed to be on the same wavelength, so I invited her to submit a story. Not only did I select it for publication, but I have since published several of her stories in other anthologies. You'll see her work in *Beltane: Ten Tales of Witchcraft, Cutlass: Ten Tales of Pirates* and *Scared: Ten Tales of Horror*.

After reading Candy Korman's (@candykorman) tweets, I grew interested in her fantasy fiction and bought a couple of her books. I enjoyed them, told her about the *Ten Tales* books, and the result was a story in *Dragon: Ten Tales of Scaly Beasts*.

When I read a delightful dragon story by L.L. Phelps (@LLPhelps1) in an ezine, I wanted to ask the author's permission to include it in my book *Dragon: Ten Tales of Fiery Beasts*. I found her on Twitter.

One day, I read a particularly insightful customer review for one of my novels on Amazon. The reviewer seemed to understand my novel better than I did! I grew curious about her, did a Twitter search and discovered that we were actually following each other. We chatted. She was looking for a writing prompt; I suggested she write about 'witchcraft'. You can read her delightful story in my anthology *Beltane: Ten Tales of Witchcraft*.

I tweeted about my online classes for writers. One of my followers, Mark Cassell (@Mark_Cassell) signed up for the short story course. The story he wrote in that class was a perfect fit for *Dragon: Ten Tales of Fiery Beasts*. Another story by Mark Cassell will soon appear in *Cogwheels: Ten Tales of Steampunk* and I was also able to recommend him to April Grey (@aprilgreynyc) who selected one of his stories for her *Hell's Garden* anthology.

Exchanging tweets with Mohanalakshmi Rajakumar (moha_doha), I became curious about her books, downloaded the free sample of her short story collection, liked it, and asked for (and received) a review copy. I liked those stories a lot, and when I had a slot in a Ten Tales book, I invited her to submit. You can read it in *Seers: Ten Tales of Clairvoyance*.

I also made contact with steampunk author Beth Daniels (@BethDaniels1). We had been exchanging occasional tweets and retweets for a while, and when I edited *Cogwheels: Ten Tales of Steampunk*, I invited her to submit. You can read her humorous yarn in the book.

These are just a few examples where a Twitter contact led to publication. What happens more often is that I read the free sample pages of a follower's books, or ask them to send me something they've written, so I can satisfy my curiosity.

Sometimes I ask my Twitter followers if they can put me in touch with a writer whose stories I've read somewhere. Often, someone knows that writer from outside the internet group and puts us in touch.

Don't get your hopes too high. The chances of a reputable agent or publisher approaching you on Twitter and inviting you to submit are small.

On the other hand, if they are interested in publishing you, they are likely to check out your Twitter account before offering you a contract. An agent or book publisher wants to see what kind of platform you have on Twitter: do you have a large established fan base who will buy your books? Are your followers real people who take note of what you do? Or are they mostly automated accounts and therefore worthless for marketing?

Before entering a business relationship, a publisher or agent will want to know what kind of person you are, whether you'll be pleasant to work with. Your tweeting style reveals a lot: are you helpful, cooperative, considerate? Or quarrelsome, self-obsessed, rude?

Most publishers, editors and agents have many followers and follow almost nobody back. You may want to follow them anyway, or read their tweets in lists (see Chapter 11), to gain insider information.

It's okay to tweet them with questions, as long as it's the kind they can answer in a single tweet: *Are you currently open to submissions? Is the word count limit firm? Do you consider humorous stories? What's your stance on characters using swearwords?*

Thank them for their reply.

WHAT NOT TO DO

Don't promote your books to other writers. They are your colleagues, not your target audience (unless, like me, you write books for writers).

Don't get sucked into large-scale swaps of promotional favours. If you tweet and retweet a lot of promos for other people, it soon becomes tedious for your followers, and they stop paying attention.

Beware especially the retweet cartels, where dozens of writers continually retweet one another's 'buy my book' tweets, and few if any real people read them. Instead, help out your colleagues on an occasional basis – when they have just launched a book or are offering their novel free for five days – and do this only if this is the kind of book your followers would enjoy.

Don't pester agents and publishers. Twitter is not the place to push your manuscript. At best, they'll ignore you. At worst, they'll put your name on a list of authors to avoid.

MISTAKES I MADE AND LEARNT FROM

In my first year on Twitter, I got carried away with 'mutual promotion' arrangements. I would tweet about other authors' books, and in return, they tweeted about mine. I also posted hundreds of promo retweets every day. 'Wow!' I thought. 'My books get mentioned in so many tweets, and my own tweets get retweeted so much – surely my book sales will soar! And I'm helping other authors, too.'

After a few months, I saw the reality: Although our promo tweets were multiplying rapidly and flitting all over the Twitterverse, nobody paid much attention to them. Instead, our followers found them tedious and tuned them out.

Now I tweet promos (my own and other writers') sparingly. I'm careful about my retweet favours. I'll still help promote a special offer or launch occasionally, but I no longer retweet hundreds of promos every day. I also help promote only books that appeal to most of my followers and stay clear of those that are likely to offend, such as extreme adult fiction with graphic pictures attached.

Sometimes I regret that I didn't create a list of people who have been helpful to me, so that I can return the favour one day. But all considered, I prefer to help whom I can, when I can, instead of keeping quid pro quo accounts. The people whom I help may not be the ones who are helping me – but overall, it's good karma for all of us and makes Twitter a pleasant place.

CHAPTER 14: MULTIPLE ACCOUNTS

If you wish, you can have several Twitter accounts. It's legitimate, and it can be useful and fun.

WHY HAVE SEVERAL ACCOUNTS?

Here are some reasons why you may choose to have more than one Twitter persona.

* A backup account can be useful, in case your main account gets temporarily suspended or you hit your daily tweeting limit just when you need to post an urgent message.

* Keep your author persona and private persona separate. Use one account to correspond with publishers and fans, and another for chatting with friends and family.

* Maintain the secret of your 'double life'. If you're a school teacher by day, and a steamy romance author by night, it's best not to mix these roles in the social media.

* If you write under different pen names, you may want a Twitter account in each name.

* Some people open Twitter accounts in the name of their pet. It can be fun composing tweets in the style of your dog or cat.

* The main characters of your novel can have their own Twitter accounts. Few people want to read tweets by fictional characters – except famous fictional characters from their favourite novels – so don't expect much promotional benefit from this. However, you'll gain many insights into your characters once you start tweeting about their lives and in their voices.

* If you want to manipulate popularity-measuring programmes, you can easily give yourself a boost by retweeting your tweets from multiple accounts. Just don't mistake the increased ranking for genuine popularity.

THE BASICS

Twitter allows the creation of multiple accounts, so you need not have any qualms.

Open the additional accounts the same way you opened the first one. Each account needs its own email address. You may want to use a free mail server such as Gmail or Yahoo to create a series of email addresses, ideally containing the name of the Twitter account.

You also need a date of birth and password for each.

To follow people or to tweet, you need to be logged into that account. Twitter allows you to log into only one account at a time, so you'll be constantly logging in and out. Apps like TweetDeck make the juggling easier, but juggling multiple accounts eats up a lot of time.

You need to decide whether or not be frank about having multiple accounts. I'm honest about mine – but you may have reason to hide your secret identity.

WHAT NOT TO DO

Don't run more accounts than you have time to manage. If it gets too much, stop doing it.

When replying to tweets, make sure you're replying from the correct account. Mistakes happen easily, leading to confusion, embarrassment – or even to being outed!

Some authors create multiple accounts, pretending to be their own fans, telling one another what a wonderful novel they've just read. These fake fan tweets don't fool anyone. You'll appear stupid and dishonest. Don't waste your credibility.

Don't spend more time than you can afford. Managing multiple accounts, writing tweets and interacting with followers, takes far more time than you probably imagine.

Don't automate your accounts. If you don't have time to maintain them properly, it's tempting to use an app to do the following, tweeting and retweeting for you. You can subscribe to services that will churn out tweets from those accounts for you, and retweet them endlessly from one account to another. However, this is pointless – because nobody will pay any notice. The only recipients are other people's fake accounts.

ADVANCED STRATEGIES

If you want to budget your social media time and energy, stick to just one account.

MISTAKES I MADE AND LEARNT FROM

In my first year on Twitter, I was so excited by my success that I wanted to replicate it. I created several accounts. To make them interesting and believable, I invented a personality, backstory and tweeting style for each of them.

For example, @FrancoFolly was a nerdy type who waxed lyrical about the algorithm of seashells, adored fractal art and read science fiction. @Calamity Cass was a quiet introvert who kept cats, enjoyed historical re-enactments, and wanted to make a mediaeval costume. @MessaLina10 was a writer given to cranky tweets and sarcastic replies. @Karolinka was a tree-hugging pacifist who studied Buddhism.

I had those characters interact with one another. This required keeping detailed charts of who had said what, who liked which books and films, lived where, feared what, admired whom and habitually used which words, as well as what was their standard punctuation mode. It also took a lot of logging in and out.

The characters also retweeted one another, awarded one another K+ points at Klout (a popularity-measuring app, see Chapter 27) and so on.

It was fun. But it was a huge time drain.

Eventually, I realised that I had spent hundreds of hours inventing characters and writing dialogue – and if I had applied this to fiction writing, I would have completed several stories.

All it gained me was – nothing. The witty exchanges remained unread, because most of the followers were other people's automated accounts. The few genuine people who followed them were following my main account as well, so I could reach them that way.

I didn't close the accounts. They came in handy when I wanted to experiment with apps and try out new strategies. This way, I could even do things I suspected were stupid – such as auto-tweeting and auto-retweeting – without cheapening my main account and losing my real followers' respect. Some of my 'What Not To Do' advice is based on what I learnt from those experiments.

On one occasion I was glad I had multiple accounts. During a TwitterParty (see Chapter 19), I hit the maximum tweet limit for the day. The party was in full swing, people chatted with me, and suddenly I could not even tweet a reply. Rats! Fortunately, I had another account I could use. Quickly, I logged out of my main account, logged in as @StormDancer_, explained the situation and carried on partying.

Another unexpected benefit: I can see which seemingly personal messages addressed to me are automated fakes, because the identical tweet is sent to all my accounts.

CHAPTER 15: SURVEYS AND RESEARCH

Twitter is a great place for writers to get information and opinions fast. I have used it for many informal surveys and simple research.

SURVEYS

Whenever you want quick feedback on something, ask your Twitter followers. The questions need to be phrased so they can be answered in a few words.

The ideal question, I find, is one which offers a choice. For example:
Which of these versions for my new book cover do you prefer – right or left? (attach a picture showing both covers).
Which book title do you prefer - 'Vanishing Vampire' or 'The Vampire Vanishes'?

Among the replies, usually a clear favourite emerges.

Avoid asking questions such as, *Do you like my new book cover?* or *Is this a good title for my novella?* because people will only respond if they can give you a positive affirmation that yes, your book cover or title is great. Courtesy compels those who dislike it to keep silent.

When I decided to replace the covers for my series of *Writer's Craft* books, the artist sent me two versions. I showed both to my Twitter followers, most of whom are writers, and thus the 'target audience' for these books. I received dozens of opinions – half preferring one, half the other. When I asked what it was people liked about their favourite, I discovered that each version had a specific feature that appealed. I told the artist about this, and she came up with a third version that combined those advantages – and now my followers were unanimous that this was the best. So when you look at the covers of my *Writer's Craft* series (including *Twitter for Writers*), you see what my Twitter followers have chosen.

I had long planned an anthology of dragon stories for the *Ten Tales* series. I had a cover picture, and the working title was *Dragon: Ten Tales of Scaly Beasts.* When the time came to choose authors and stories, I asked my Twitter followers – many of whom are ardent lovers of fantasy fiction – what kind of dragon stories they would enjoy reading most. To my surprise, many mentioned the appeal of fire-breathing. With this in mind, I selected stories where dragons breathed fire. I also changed the book cover from green to red, chose a flame-themed font, and changed the title to *Dragon: Ten Tales of Fiery Beasts.*

For this kind of survey to work, you need followers who have an interest in the subject. I received valuable feedback because my followers were fantasy fiction lovers and writers keen to improve their craft – exactly the kind of people to whom I wanted my books to appeal.

If Suzie Scrybe's followers are vampire fiction fans, their opinions on a vampire novella title count, and if Franco Folly has an audience of dog owners, their choice of the best cover for a puppy training book matters.

Thank the people who gave their views, either individually (if there were only a few answers) or in a general way, perhaps combined with the result of the survey: *Thanks everyone who voted for the book cover versions. This has been very helpful. Most (not all) preferred version B.*

RESEARCH

While you're writing, you may suddenly need a piece of information. Wikipedia and other online resources are great for facts, but for that authentic flavour, nothing beats personal experience. Ask your followers if they've ever done that, and what it felt like.

Has anyone ever been close to starvation? What's it like? #amwriting #research.

The hashtags #amwriting and #research explain why you ask. Other writers are always happy to help a colleague, readers find it exciting to help an author, and your fans will be giddy with delight knowing they've contributed to your next book.

The advantage of asking your Twitter followers is that you get replies almost immediately. The disadvantage is that a tweet doesn't have much room for detail. You may want to follow up by email.

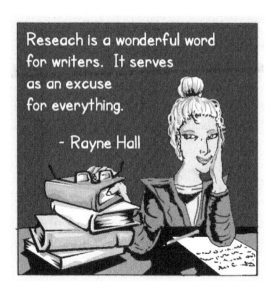

Reseach is a wonderful word for writers. It serves as an excuse for everything.

- Rayne Hall

WHAT NOT TO DO

Don't treat responses to your informal surveys as statistically significant samples in the academic sense. There's too much randomness involved, depending on who happens to read your tweet and feels like responding.

Don't expect meaningful replies if your followers are automated accounts.

ADVANCED STRATEGIES

Post the same question – with slightly altered wording – several times during the day, to get responses from people who log onto Twitter at different times.

Once people have contributed their opinion or experience, they often develop an interest in the project and want it to succeed. If the project is a book, they may await its release eagerly. They may buy it, review it, talk about it or retweet your publication announcements.

CHAPTER 16: BUILDING A QUALITY PLATFORM

Having many followers is good, but only if they read your tweets and are interested in what you say.

Getting many junk followers is easy. If you want, you can get 100,000 followers fast. But if they pay no attention, don't care about your topics or have automated their accounts, they are useless to you. A single genuine follower is worth far more than 100,000 automated followers.

Don't get sucked into the race for great follower numbers. Instead, attract quality followers who read your tweets. This is called 'building a platform'.

THE IDEAL FOLLOWERS

* They share your interests, for example, reading or writing.

* They enjoy reading the kind of books you write. In marketing terms, they are your 'target audience'.

* They read your tweets – not 24/7, of course, but now and then.

* They respond to your tweets, ask and answer questions, chat with you. In marketing terms, they 'engage'.

* They use little or no automation for their Twitter account.

* They favourite or retweet only tweets they genuinely like, not with an app that favourites randomly or automatically retweets people who retweet them.

* Their own followers are also mostly genuine people.

HOW TO ATTRACT THEM

Tweet about the subjects of interest to these people. Since they are the target audience for your books, talk about the subject matter of your books – vampires, puppies, history, time travel, daffodils. Use hashtags for these keywords.

Chat with your followers about these topics. This will draw eavesdroppers and lead to new followers.

Look for other people's tweets – especially genuine conversations – containing the hashtagged keywords. Join those chats.

Share URLs to news articles, blog posts and websites of interest to your followers, especially about your subjects. Hashtag them.

Create value content. What kind of tweet would your target audience enjoy? Can you share jokes or offer useful tips? My target audience is writers. I post funny cartoon memes about a writer's life, as well as #writetip and #indiepubtip tweets. Suzie Scrybe might post funny vampire cartoons, while Franco Folly could tweet dog training tips. This is what marketing professionals call 'content marketing'.

Post as few promotional tweets as possible. The less you promote, the more attractive you become. Churning out promos drives away the kind of people you need to attract.

Instead, let people become curious about you. Many people who chat with me or who eavesdrop on my chats want to find out about me. They check my profile, then look up my books. Often, they buy my books. I know this, because they tell me. Some actually buy my books simply because they want to support the rare writer who doesn't flood them with promos!

"Some people gain time by automating their Twitter accounts. I gain attention by being real."
- Rayne Hall

Establish yourself as the person on Twitter to answer questions or with whom to chat about that topic. Once your name and the topic are firmly connected in people's minds, they are more likely to buy your book than anyone else's.

Writers are the target audience for my Writer's Craft books. I'm happy to answer questions about writing, publishing and related topics, and I'm delighted when people on Twitter advise one another, "Ask @RayneHall. She'll know the answer."

Suzie Scrybe might aim to become the go-to person for vampirical matters, while Franco Folly would answer dog-related questions. Without overt promotion, this will help them sell their vampire romances and puppy training books. For what subject could you become the helpful expert?

WHAT NOT TO DO

If you post a lot of promotional/advertising tweets, the genuine people will unfollow or ignore you.

This means, you won't have an audience (platform). Tweeting promotions when nobody listens is pointless.

ADVANCED STRATEGIES

Nothing attracts quality followers as much as live chat about their favourite topics. Enlist the help of a couple of friends – writers of the same genre are ideal – and chat about vampires, dogs, time travel, daffodils or whatever you write about. Use the technique of the full stop before the first user name to facilitate widespread eavesdropping (See Chapter 8). Refrain from any mention of your books – you need to impress the importance of this on your friends - but mention the keywords often, and hashtag them. Other people will soon join the chat which will become lively. Make the most of this by favouriting and retweeting many tweets from this conversation. If you want to invest your social media time productively, this is an excellent strategy. Do it as often as your time allows.

CHAPTER 17: PROMOTING YOUR BOOK

Whenever I read someone's claims that 'Twitter is useless for book promotion,' I laugh. These people are going about it the wrong way.

Twitter is an excellent medium for promoting books. It certainly works for me – better than any other social media, better than advertising, better than anything else I have tried.

In this chapter, I'm showing examples of my own promotional tweets. This is not to promote my books to you, but to provide you with models of successful tweets on which to model your own.

WHAT NOT TO DO

Some people churn out promotional tweets – *Have you bought my book yet? If not, here's your opportunity. You will love this book! Absolutely unputdownable! Must read! Buy now!!!!!!*

They expect people who see this tweet to rush out and buy the book – and are surprised if that doesn't happen.

All day long we get bombarded with advertising – radio, newspapers, websites, posters etc. all scream at us, Buy this!' Our minds have become conditioned to ignore advertising. Promotional tweets abound on Twitter. They account for at least 90% of tweets – and sometimes near 100%.

Promos are just annoying noise; people tune them out. By adding to the noise, you achieve nothing.

Don't address your promos to individual people. (*@SuzieScrybe My new book is out. You'll love it! Buy it here...*) This is intrusive spam and annoys people greatly; many will block you for spamming.

STRATEGY

Before you start promoting your books, you need a platform – followers who read your tweets and are interested in what you say. Unless people pay attention, your promotion will simply evaporate in the ether. Devote time and effort to building your platform (see Chapter 16), then start promoting.

Send more helpful, funny, entertaining, interactive tweets than promos. If your followers enjoy reading your tweets, they'll conclude that your books may be fun to read, too – and this is what sells your books.

By all means, tweet about your books. Once your followers are hooked on your tweets, they'll be open to what else you have to offer. But tweet fewer promos than other stuff.

How many promos should you tweet?

Some people set 'rules' what ratio of promo tweets is acceptable. Some say 20%, others 40% or 60%. Don't bother adhering to such rules – I certainly don't. Promote books when it makes sense to promote them, which will be more during some times than others. For example, when you've just launched a new novel, when your book is free for a few days or when you offer a discount price, it makes sense to tweet more about it than usual.

I've found that the fewer promos I tweet overall, the more attention people pay to all my tweets - including the promos. I've experimented with this extensively, and the pattern is clear. Promote sparingly, and your promotion gets noticed. Promote excessively, and your promotion gets ignored.

Make your promo tweets interesting. Use a hashtag or two - especially the words that attract your target audience. When Franco Folly promotes his dog training books, it helps to mention #dogs or #puppies. Suzie Scrybe should try to include #vampire or #vampires.

Avoid hashtag diarrhoea (see Chapter 6) and the kind of hashtag that smacks of tedious advertising such as #bookplugs and #mustbuy.

Use link shorteners, especially for Amazon (see Chapter 23).

Vary your promo tweets to keep them interesting. Here are some ideas.

BASIC PROMO TWEETS

Simply say what your book is about or what its genre is, preferably with a hashtag, possibly phrased as a question. Give the title and a URL to the book's product page on a major sales site such as Amazon. If possible, attach a picture of the full or partial cover (see Chapter 7).

Avoid hyperbole and exclamation marks. Use capitals sparingly or not at all. Don't space them out over many lines.

This type of tweet inspires trust because of its honest simplicity. It works well if you have already built a good relationship with your followers.

Here are some examples of my own tweets of this type:

For fantasy & paranormal writers: WRITING ABOUT MAGIC for #Kindle. viewBook.at/B00CQWXSQI pic.twitter.com/OELeOJqXpZ #writing

Dark-epic fantasy novel "Storm Dancer". Caution: not for the faint of heart. #Kindle viewBook.at/B005MJFV58 pic.twitter.com/rPwfmOLMUQ

Exciting fantasy stories by 10 authors http://myBook.to/DragonTales DRAGON: TEN TALES OF FIERY BEASTS pic.twitter.com/qNVW6oaG5v

Do you like #vampires? "Bites: Ten Tales of Vampires" 10 stories, 10 authors. Kindle http://ow.ly/9DByf pic.twitter.com/Sx8l4v16qF

Creepy, atmospheric, unsettling (not gory): "Thirty Scary Tales" #Kindle http://viewBook.at/30ScaryTales pic.twitter.com/JPoYaNEI68

For authors: "The Word-Loss Diet" Powerful self-editing techniques http://viewBook.at/B00AWA7XEE #Kindle pic.twitter.com/9AtHhalqlA

Writers - do you want to make your fights realistic&
exciting? WRITING FIGHT SCENES Smashwords:
http://dld.bz/dk2Mh

MINI-EXCERPTS

Of all promotional tweets, this type is the most successful in selling fiction.

Go through your book, select pithy sentences, and turn them into tweets. The challenge is to find sentences that give a flavour of the book's content and your writing style, arouse curiosity, and are short enough to fit into tweets while still leaving room for the title and the URL. Find at least ten, more if you can. For *Storm Dancer*, I have about three hundred. The variety creates curiosity, constantly teasing your followers with a new bite until they crave the whole book.

When I tweet my mini-excerpts, followers often tell me that they love a certain phrase, or that they're going to buy the book. Here are the most successful mini-excerpts of Storm Dancer:

Already, the air soaked up heat, and the pale sky stretched taut like the skin of a clay-drum. Storm Dancer viewBook.at/B005MJFV58

"I need men with courage and sense who can drum and aren't afraid of foreign magic." Storm Dancer viewBook.at/B005MJFV58

Her smile warmed his chest, but he dared not let it reach his heart, because he was not worthy of her. Storm Dancer viewBook.at/B005MJFV58

The air simmered with suspicion and dangerous desires. Storm Dancer viewBook.at/B005MJFV58

He had to tell her the truth about himself, but the words stuck in his throat. Storm Dancer viewBook.at/B005MJFV58 viewBook.at/B005MJFV58

Afternoon light filtered through filigree lattices, dipping Teruma's study into pale gold. Storm Dancer viewBook.at/B005MJFV58

With clinking cymbals and spinning fabrics, a bellydancer whirled into the room. #StormDancer viewBook.at/B005MJFV58

Although his mouth smiled, his eyes were bitter-dark like olives. #StormDancer viewBook.at/B005MJFV58

The hands were wrong: calloused, rough and ridged with old scars, they did not belong to a courtier, StormDancer viewBook.at/B005MJFV58

The rhythmic shush and crunch of the horse's hooves were the only sounds under the searing sun. Storm Dancer viewBook.at/B005MJFV58

REVIEW EXCERPTS

Look at the favourable reviews your book has received, and select excerpts to use in tweets.

Pick excerpts which give a clear idea of the book's flavour, rather than generic praise that would fit any book ("Great book, I couldn't put it down.") Make it clear that you are quoting a review, otherwise it sounds as if you're praising your own book. Fitting it all into a single tweet can be difficult.

Here are some examples:

"Magic, deceit and betrayal" review for Storm Dancer (dark epic fantasy) on Amazon viewBook.at/B005MJFV58

"Dark fantasy set against a richly developed locale" Amazon review for Storm Dancer viewBook.at/B005MJFV58

"A world reminiscent of the One Thousand and One Nights" Amazon review for Storm Dancer (dark epic fantasy) viewBook.at/B005MJFV58

"You see the shimmering heat rising from the sun-blasted terrain" review for Storm Dancer (dark epic fantasy) viewBook.at/B005MJFV58

"Magic...mind readers...belly dancing...epic battles" review for Storm Dancer (dark epic fantasy) on Amazon viewBook.at/B005MJFV58

ADVANCED STRATEGIES

When you have created effective promo tweets, compile them in a document, mix them up and save them. You can save time by using them repeatedly, perhaps spread out over a month and then starting again. Useful apps allow bulk uploading and even managing queues. However, don't get carried away and become one of those pests that promote their books non-stop. If you plan to reuse your promo tweets, it's best not to mention prices, because those may change frequently. Also check that the URLs are still correct before you recycle the tweets.

Put the URL in the middle of the tweet instead of at the end – apparently, this encourages more clicks.

Consider seasonal or topical angles for your Twitter promotions.

At the end of April and on 1 May, I promote *Beltane: Ten Tales of Witchcraft*. On Talk Like A Pirate day, I tweet about *Cutlass: Ten Tales of Pirates*. In the run-up to Halloween, I promote *Thirty Scary Tales* and *Haunted: Ten Tales of Ghosts*. During December, when people buy books as Christmas presents, I include URLs to the paperback editions, and once Christmas gets close, I suggest buying ebooks as last-minute gifts.

MISTAKES I MADE AND LEARNT FROM

Like almost everyone, I went overboard with promotional tweets for a while – but I soon discovered that this didn't bring the desired results.

CHAPTER 18: GETTING BOOK REVIEWS

Most reviewers are inundated with books and requests, and their to-read pile grows faster than they can work through it. How do you persuade reviewers to take a look at your book?

THE BASICS

Instead of contacting reviewers begging them to review your book, and waiting in the hopes that one of them will reply, simply tweet that your book is available for review.
People who are interested in the book will reply.

These are not professional reviewers, but genuine readers, so their reviews are natural and authentic. Typically, they post the reviews on their blogs and also on bookselling sites like Amazon and Barnes & Noble.

About every eight weeks, I post a tweet like this:

Would anyone like one of my ebooks for free for posting a brief review at Amazon? Storm Dancer, Writing Fight Scenes, others

Calling all writers: You can get free review copies of my Writer's Craft books if you review them on your blog, on Amazon or elsewhere

I always get several responses. We exchange email addresses by DM, and I send them the ebook, encouraging them to write an honest review about what they like and don't like about the book.

If you have built a quality platform of followers who are interested in the subjects of your books, you will get quality responses. Obviously, this doesn't work if your followers are mostly automated accounts and people who don't care about your topics.

Reviewers receive the books free – but they don't get anything else. Don't try to bribe them with payment, gifts or other incentives. Accepting a free copy doesn't place the reviewer under any obligation. They can still decide against reviewing the book, for example, if they find it's not to their taste after all.

Almost everyone who requested a review copy via Twitter actually writes a review, while elsewhere, more than half the promised reviews never happen.

Beware freeloaders who never intend to review the books they request. They request every free print book on offer and sell the pristine copies on eBay or Amazon. You can avoid this by offering ebooks only. They cost you nothing to send and have no resale value on eBay. Most Twitter users have an e-reading device. Grant requests for paperbacks only to followers who have chatted with you in the past. If you have a Twitter relationship, you know their interest in your book is genuine and they're not trying to cheat you.

Ernest Hemingway says:
"There's nothing to tweeting. All you do is sit at a laptop and bleed."

WHAT NOT TO DO

Don't request reviews from people who have just followed you. Automated DM tweets, *Thanks for following me. Please download a FREE copy of my book and review it,* annoy and won't attract reviewers.

Avoid asking the individual people you chat with for book reviews. This puts them in an awkward position if they like you but have no time or interest in your book. Making a general offer for review copies is much better; then they can speak up if they're interested.

Don't engage in review swaps. New authors are often so desperate for reviews that they form review cartels - 'I review your book if you review mine'. This frequently leads to dishonest reviews (praising each other's books, awarding five stars, often without even reading them) or hurt feelings (when one author doesn't love the other's book). It also undermines the authors' credibility. Readers who study reviews before buying books tend to check who wrote the reviews, and if they discover mutual back-scratching, they'll shun those authors.

ADVANCED STRATEGIES

Many people enjoy helping others achieve a goal. If you aim to have a specific number of reviews by a specific date, your followers may be keen to help you. I find if I ask this way, I receive more promises than actual reviews, because people are so keen to help that they forget to consider the time involved. Still, some will follow through and boost your reviews.

Phrase your tweet similar to this:

My goal: Twenty Amazon reviews for 'The Vamp Vanishes' (paranormal romance) before the end of the year. Can you help?

Bloggers are interested in seasonal or topical material for their blogs. Offer your book a few weeks before the date. For example, if you want reviews for your Christmas romance, tweet the offer in November. On Halloween, bloggers like to post reviews of scary books, so the beginning of October is a good time to tweet this.

Example:

Bloggers – would you like a free review copy of my ebook 'Thirty Scary Tales' to review on your blog for Halloween?

CHAPTER 19: HOLDING A TWITTERPARTY

A Twitterparty is a themed online event where you interact with your followers intensely. This is great for drawing attention to yourself and your books, bonding with fans, and gaining new followers.

Twitterparties are huge fun – but they require thought and preparation.

THE BASICS

Decide on a day and time that's convenient to you and when many of your followers are online. However, it may be wisest to avoid Twitter's peak times, because that's when traffic sometimes breaks down and the 'Twitter is over capacity' error message appears.

Announce it in advance, starting about a week before, and tweeting about it frequently as the event draws closer.

Who'll join my #TwitterParty on Monday? 8-9pm EST. We're celebrating the launch of my new vampire romance.

A #TwitterParty for #vampire lovers! Tomorrow, 8-9EST. Celebrate the launch of my novel 'The Vampire Vanishes'.

#TwitterParty starts in 1 hour! All are welcome. Chat, games, giveaway – and it's all about #vampires.

Prepare activities. Here are some ideas.

'Hangman' is a good game to play on Twitter, though you may have to do it without displaying the growing picture. Write the questions in advance, so you can copy-paste them quickly. Choose questions that are related to your book's content (e.g. vampires or dogs) but not about the book itself. This way, people will enjoy playing without feeling they're being promoted to.

A popular activity at my Twitterparties is my offer to answer all questions put to me – even embarrassing ones (with the exception of safety hazards such as my credit card number). This offer always gets a laugh and a lot of speculations about whether I really will answer the embarrassing questions. However, no question was ever of the kind that made me squirm. Even intimate ones ("Do you shave your nether regions?") can be answered very briefly without providing details.

At a Twitterparty for the publication anniversary of Storm Dancer, one of the novel's characters participated. The Whiteseer gave cryptic answers to people's questions. For this, I created an account with the name @WhiteSeer, and a list of fifty pre-written nonsensical utterances. What character could you use? In what way? It has to be simple, typical of that character, yet easy to grasp for people who have not yet read your novel. Create a separate account for the character, and use TweetDeck to flip between the accounts fast.

Find suitable music to play in the background, something related to your novel's genre or subject. The easiest way to do this is to tweet a link to a musical YouTube video. This provides the right mood.

Pictures help a lot. You can tweet links, but it's better if you attach the actual pictures in a way that doesn't require clicking. For instructions on how to do this, see Chapter 7. When attaching pictures, make sure you have the permission of the copyright owner. A good site is DeviantArt where artists display their work, though you need to sign up for an account to contact them. Many are keen to get exposure, and will happily give permission as long as you attribute the picture to them. You can also use stock photos from sites like DreamsTime, DepositPhotos and ShutterStock. They usually offer some photos for free use, while they charge a fee for the rest. If you decide to purchase the right to use photos, consider what other uses you might have for them, either on Twitter or elsewhere.

Decide on a hashtag to use. This should be your book title, perhaps in a shortened form, such as #VampVanishes. At the start of the Twitterparty, and whenever a new arrival joins, tell them to use 'Search', type in the hashtag, and then click 'All'. This will show all tweets containing the hashtag as they get posted – basically, the whole party.

Tell participants to use the hashtag in their tweets, and remind them. When the party is in full swing, people tend to forget the hashtag.

Additional hashtags can be useful, but they use up tweet space. If every tweet contains the hashtags #TwitterParty #BookLaunch #VampVanishes #Vampire, there's little room left for the actual text. Stick to the one recurring hashtag, but when you happen to use a key word (e.g. 'vampire') in your text, hashtag it.

Whenever someone asks a question, reply immediately. Interaction is the key to a successful TwitterParty. Draw people out by asking questions.

Once several people have joined the chats, many of the 140 characters get used up by a string of usernames, leaving little room for text:

.@SuzieScrybe @FrancoFolly @RayneHall @MessaLina10 @Calamity_Cass @Book_Thrills @StormDancer_ @VictorGent No

When chats get strangled this way, simply delete some of the usernames. They will still receive the tweets because they are following the hashtag.

Type out as many tweets as possible in advance. Think about what kind of tweets you may need, and have them at hand to copy/paste. The pace of a Twitterparty is very fast – it feels like a race, leaving you breathless and struggling to keep up. You simply won't have time to type every tweet, and it helps to have some pre-written ones.

Try not to 'sell' your book. This would drive people away. Instead, give people a fun experience and a promo-free flavour of what's in the book. Then they'll remember your book title and the associated pleasure.

An hour is a good scheduled length for a Twitterparty. Few people want to spend more – although in practice, my Twitterparties were always so much fun that some of us kept going much longer.

I find that most people who participate in my Twitterparties do so spontaneously – they see something is going on and want to join the fun. A few are fans and friends who put the date in their diary.

WHAT NOT TO DO

Don't use up your tweet allowance. Twitter limits how many updates (tweets) you can send per day (see Chapter 24). To avoid running out of tweets in the middle of the party, tweet sparingly in the hours before.

Don't hijack someone else's party. When @SuzieScrybe throws a party to celebrate her book *The Vamp Vanishes*, don't butt in with advertising for your own vampire novel.

ADVANCED STRATEGIES

Attract eavesdroppers by placing a full stop before the first user name. Encourage the other participants to do the same.

Favourite and retweet (see Chapter 3) as many tweets as possible. This spreads the party fun and pulls in more and more party guests.

Recruit a couple of friends who're willing to commit in advance. Brief them about using the hashtag and the full stop. Ask them to engage with participants, to favourite and retweet.

If you have a budget for social media marketing, the Twitterparty is an occasion when you may want to spend a little money. Hire someone for an hour to join the party, to ask questions, tweet and retweet. They need to have their own account and some Twitter experience, though not necessarily many followers. A good place to hire someone is Elance.com.

If your Twitterparty is very successful, your novel title may become a trending hashtag. This happens very rarely, yet I have achieved it several times. At my very first Twitterparty, #StormDancer became the number two trending topic worldwide for several hours. I didn't realise at the time what a miraculous achievement this was - but when I mentioned it to social media marketing professionals, they gasped. They dreamed of getting a hashtag trending, worked hard to attain it but never succeeded - and here I was, accomplishing the miracle by having fun.

To make the hashtag a trending topic, get many people to join the party, and encourage them to retweet a lot.

Create a backup account, just in case problems occur with your main one.

MISTAKES I MADE AND LEARNT FROM

During my first Twitterparty, I planned many activities, with lots of games and contests arranged in a detailed schedule – and we didn't have time for them. Time ran out while we were still playing the first game. Now I keep things simple, holding just one game and keeping one spare activity in readiness in case it's needed.

I was so busy promoting my forthcoming Twitterparty that I constantly tweeted *Twitterparty starts in 7 hours. Twitterparty starts in 25 minutes.* During the party, I naturally tweeted a lot, and I also retweeted everything. Then suddenly while the party was in full swing, Twitter informed me that I had reached my daily limit and could not tweet any more! Fortunately, I had another, little-used account I could log into. I explained the situation and continued partying. Nowadays, I budget my tweets carefully, tweeting very little on the actual day until the party begins.

CHAPTER 20: GIVEAWAYS AND CONTESTS

Contests and giveaways are great ways to gain attention on Twitter and exposure for your book.

GIVEAWAYS

Offer your book (or some other prize) free – either to everyone who requests it within a certain timespan, or draw several winners from among the applicants.

This is a simple way of organising a giveaway, and works especially well for ebooks.

You need a substantial platform of many followers who are interested in the prize. Announce the giveaway beforehand, for example:

When I post my 100,000th tweet (soon) I'll hold a giveaway for my forthcoming book 'Twitter for Writers

Giveaway starts in 1 hour – ebook 'The Vamp Vanishes' by Suzie Scrybe. Watch this space.

Make it easy for people to apply, perhaps by replying to your tweet:

Free ebook 'The Vamp Vanishes' (vampire romance) to everyone who replies to this tweet within 15 minutes.

I found it useful to ask for retweets instead of replies, because this spreads the word beyond your own followers:

Everyone who retweets this in the next 10 minutes gets my next ebook 'Twitter for Writers' by Rayne Hall free. pic.twitter.com/Tt21y6sR6B

If offering a free item to everyone who applies, you need to cap your offer somehow – perhaps say that only 100 books are available, or that the giveaway ends at a specific time. Otherwise you may have to send out thousands of prizes, which may exceed what you can afford.

I have only ever given away ebooks which cost me nothing, although it took time to get all the winners' email addresses and send the books out.

When setting a time limit, interpret it generously, and award the prizes to those whose tweets arrive late. Their tweets may have been held up in the process, or they may only just have seen the giveaway and would really, really like to read your book.

Don't award prizes based on the number of tweets or retweets people generate for you: this would clog the system with meaningless identical tweets and is against Twitter rules.

William Shakespeare says:
"Is this a tweet I see before me?"

CONTESTS

Invite your followers to create something in tweet-length – perhaps a one-sentence story or a haiku on a given theme. Make the theme something related to your book.

Run the contest for one or two days only.

Announce the contest at least a week in advance, but reveal the actual rules and theme on the day.

Contest rules need to be clear. Since they don't fit into a tweet, create a page on your (or a friend's) website or blog. This page needs to specify the following:

* Who may participate? (I suggest 'everyone with a Twitter account', 'excluding the judges and their families' and perhaps 'over 18s only')
* Are multiple entries accepted? (I always allow them. Some people have enormous fun writing a dozen funny tweets.)
* How should participants present their entry? (I suggest: addressed to your user name and with a specific hashtag such as #vampirecontest)
* Who are the judges? (It's a legal requirement in many countries that the judge and the sponsor/organiser must not be the same person, so ask some friends to act as a judging panel in return for the publicity)
* What are the prizes? (I offer mostly ebooks, but I have also offered in-depth critiques for a story or scene by the winner, and I promise to retweet the winning entries.)
* When does the contest end?
* How, when and where will the winners be announced?

You can tweet the list of judges. This gives exposure to them and draws attention to your contest:

The Tweet Writing Contest judges will be: @KOMcLaughlin @JohnBlackport   @LarisaWalk   @jb121jonathan @douglaskolacki http://buff.ly/14E3rfY

My contests were tweet-writing contests. On one occasion, participants had to write one sentence containing the word 'Cauldron' - this was to promote the book *Beltane: Ten Tales of Witchcraft*. Another time, I asked for a sentence inspired by the cover of *Storm Dancer*.

Amazingly, what winners valued most was to have their success announced by tweet and their winning entries retweeted by the judges and me.

When organising a contest, you need to comply with Twitter's contest rules. They change from time to time, so check the latest version. https://support.twitter.com/articles/68877-guidelines-for-contests-on-twitter

WHAT NOT TO DO

Don't offer physical prizes (such as paperbacks) that require shipping. If the winners live in other countries, the cost of postage can be enormous. Digital prizes (such as ebooks) are more practical.

Avoid valuable prizes that may tempt people to launch legal disputes.

Don't select the giveaway winners or judge the contest entries yourself. Use a random selector app for the giveaway and appoint an independent judge for your contest.

Stay clear of contests and prizes that are legally problematic (such as explicit erotica involving children) and bear in mind that Twitter members live in different countries with different laws. If in doubt, get legal advice.

ADVANCED STRATEGIES

Consider holding a contest or giveaway on a day that's related to your subject. For example, if the contest is for a tweet-length ghost story to promote your spooky novel, schedule it for the days before Halloween. This may get you additional publicity, especially if you use a seasonal trending hashtag in the announcements.

MISTAKES I'VE MADE AND LEARNT FROM

Fearing that things might get out of hand, I was over-cautious with my giveaways, saying 'everyone who retweets this in the next ten minutes wins a prize' - but the event really gained momentum at the end of the ten minutes and would probably have taken off in a big way had I allowed a full hour. It never got out of hand.

CHAPTER 21 GOING VIRAL

Sometimes, a tweet becomes so popular, it gets retweeted over and over, spreading like a benign virus all over the Twitterverse. If this happens to one of yours, celebrate!

Every marketer wants their tweets to go viral, but few achieve this. Several of mine have gone viral, reaching several hundred thousand people.

You can try it with yours. I can give you some tips, although there is no guaranteed recipe for success.

First, you need a platform – a large number of followers who read your tweets. If your followers are few, or if they're mostly automated accounts, it won't work.

Next, you need content. Only interesting content goes viral. If you expect the Twitterverse to get excited about a tweet *Buy my wonderful book for 99c*, you're kidding yourself.

Create tweets that appeal to your followers, the kind that makes them think, 'Wow, this is cool! I want to share this with my followers'.

In my experience, this works best when I tweet something that many others secretly think but don't dare to say aloud, when it addresses people's quiet hopes or pent-up frustrations, or when they recognise their own situation.

Humour works. Most tweets that go viral are funny. People like a laugh, and they like sharing a laugh. Visual content (pictures or videos) encourages virality.

Here are a couple of my cartoons that went viral, getting a huge number of responses, favourites and retweets among the writing community. Note that they are visual, funny and relevant to my followers (most of whom are writers) and present a situation they recognise.

The average indie-published author earns more than the average unpublished author.

- Rayne Hall

Although Twitter shows how often a tweet has been retweeted with the 'retweet' button, the real number is often much bigger. Many people use other retweeting methods, for example the 'old style' retweeting where the tweet appears to be sent from their account, prefaced with 'RT user name', and some modify the tweets before they retweet them. These types of retweets aren't included in the simple statistics.

Great content often gets removed from the original tweet. Your picture or video may go viral – but without your tweet attached. Make sure the content contains your name or book title somewhere, otherwise the effect is wasted. I always include my name in the pithy comments I post, and when it's a cartoon without text, I ask the cartoonists to include one of my books in the picture.

WHAT NOT TO DO

Don't pay for 'viral tweeting' services that promise to make your tweets go viral. They retweet your tweet from many automated accounts which are followed by other automated accounts, so it looks like something big is happening – but in reality, nobody pays attention to those tweets. Virality is something money can't buy.

ADVANCED STRATEGIES

Find out when most of your followers are online and actively reading your tweets. This is a good time to post a tweet you hope to make viral.

Ask friends to retweet this particular tweet – real friends with real accounts and real followers, not auto-retweeters. Your friends will probably be glad to do you the favour, as long as you don't ask it often. I suggest you wait to see how the tweet is doing on its own. Once it's gained a substantial number of retweets (say, 50 or so), it's on the brink of going viral, and that's when it's worth enlisting your friends' support.

CHAPTER 22: SHOUTOUTS

When you tell your followers about another person, that's called a 'shoutout'. Shoutouts are a useful service, because they connect like-minded people.

THE BASICS

You can mention a single person in a tweet:

Many of my #Writing and #Cats With #Books cartoons were created by illustrator Hanna-Riikka (@DoNichiArt) pic.twitter.com/foSrwWb0Qc

More often, shoutouts feature a group of people:

Authors featured in 'Spells: Ten Tales of Magic': @daviddlevine   @bookworm0753   @douglaskolacki @JeffreySHargett

Find a theme for your shoutout tweet – for example, 'Romance Readers', 'Book Reviewers', 'Science Fiction Writers', 'Indie Authors' - and choose several people to mention. As a favour to your followers, be picky about who you include in your shoutout lists. These should be people you follow, whose tweets you find worth reading, not spammers, trolls, promo churners or automated accounts.

You can post a shoutout anytime. However, Friday is a traditional day for recommending people to follow; use the hashtag #followfriday or #ff. On Wednesdays, shoutouts for writers are popular, using the hashtag #ww.

Other people's shoutouts are a good source for finding people to follow. Pay attention, and you'll discover like-minded people with whom you can network.

WHAT NOT TO DO

Don't post shoutouts containing lots of user names without a unifying theme.

Don't obsess over how often you can get your name mentioned in shoutouts. Some people form shoutout cartels, where every member mentions all the others. Then everyone retweets all the shoutouts, and replies to every shoutout mention with a thank-you tweet, which in turn gets retweeted by everyone else.

This is how it looks:

@FrancoFolly tweets: #ff *@SuzieScrybe* *@MessaLina10* *@Calamity_Cass* *@Book_Thrills* *@StormDancer_* *@VictorGent*

Everyone in this group posts a near-identical tweet, and everyone retweets it.

@Suzie Scrybe replies: *.@FrancoFolly* *@SuzieScrybe* *@MessaLina10* *@Calamity_Cass* *@Book_Thrills* *@StormDancer_* *@VictorGent Thank you for the shoutout*

All the others also thank everyone else, and everyone retweets the thanks. By the time they have all responded with 'you're welcome', this has generated a hundred meaningless tweets that clutter up their followers' timelines and are of no use to anyone.

ADVANCED STRATEGIES

Create shoutouts with a theme that's related to your novel. For example, Suzie Scrybe might have shoutouts about 'Twilight Fans', 'Vampire Fiction Writers' and 'Vampire Movie Lovers', while Franco Folly might compile 'Dog Owners', 'Dog Trainers' and 'Animal Rescue Shelters'.

Once you've created a shoutout tweet, you can use it repeatedly, perhaps every Friday or once a month. However, check that it is still up-to-date, because people leave Twitter, get suspended, change their usernames or automate their accounts and are no longer worth following. Keeping shoutouts current takes more work than you may imagine.

MISTAKES I MADE AND LEARNT FROM

In my early days on Twitter, I created lots of shoutouts. I studied my followers' profiles and grouped them into subjects, especially by genre, such as 'Vampire Writers', 'Romance Writers', 'Horror Writers' and so on. This was appreciated (at the time, very few people were providing this service) and probably boosted my popularity. However, this took an enormous amount of time, sorting, copying, compiling, formatting, scheduling those tweets, and above all, keeping them up-to-date. Every week, some of the usernames became dead accounts, which made me look foolish for recommending them, and some showed such appalling behaviour that I felt bad having suggested them. I believe I spent around three hours per week just updating the shoutouts. While this was a useful service for my followers, I decided I could not really afford to spend this time.

Now I run very few shoutouts, mostly for writers who followback writers, members of the Procrastinating Writers Club, and authors whose stories I published in the Ten Tales books.

CHAPTER 23: SHORTENING LINKS

Since tweets have to be short, there often simply isn't room for a full URL, let alone several.
This chapter shows some ways around this.

THE BASICS

When you post a link in a tweet, Twitter will automatically shorten it, so it shows only the beginning but functions fully when someone clicks on it.

However, this doesn't always work when you want to add a second URL, and it doesn't work at all if someone copies and pastes the tweet elsewhere.

Use a link-shortening service to create shorter links that fit comfortably into a tweet. These services are free, and there are many of them to choose from. The services change names, features and ownership frequently, so I'm not recommending specific ones. However, you can search for 'Link shortening' or 'URL shortener' and a number of options come up. Many of them end with '.ly' such as Bit.ly and Buff.ly.

They are easy to use. You paste your full URL into the box, and the service creates a very short URL for you to use instead. Some of them even track how often the link gets clicked, which can be useful information.

Pick one where the URLs don't expire. Create short links to all your books on all sales sites (e.g. Barnes & Noble, Smashwords), and also to your website and other pages you want to tweet frequently.

With link shorteners, you can often fit two URLS into a single tweet:

Do you like #fantasy stories? SPELLS: TEN TALES OF MAGIC by 10 authors. #Kindle:viewBook.at/B009YKBT34 #Nook: http://dld.bz/cHKnA

Writing Fight Scenes, practical guide for authors. Kindle: http://dld.bz/cUfD2 IiTunes: http://dld.bz/cQHKr #writing

WRITING SCARY SCENES ebook for authors #Kindle: viewBook.at/B008IEJTSE #Smashwords: http://buff.ly/NdmyqZ pic.twitter.com/yzyJjuREvE

ADVANCED STRATEGIES

Here is a nifty trick for authors with books on Amazon.

Amazon has several separate websites for customers in different countries, and they cannot buy ebooks from any but their national sites. This means your followers in the US can buy your book only if you give the link to the book's product page on Amazon.com, while the Britons need the link to Amazon.co.uk. Readers in Japan, Brazil, Canada, Germany, Italy, France, Spain, Australia and India require yet other URLs.

The solution is to create a link that will open the book's product page in the national Amazon of the person who clicks the link. This way, you need only a single URL for Amazon customers all over the world.

Try these links and see it for yourself. They will show you the book in the Amazon of your region.

Storm Dancer: viewBook.at/B005MJFV58
Writing Fight Scenes: viewBook.at/B005MJFVS0
Thirty Scary Tales: viewBook.at/30ScaryTales
Dragon: Ten Tales of Fiery Beasts
http://myBook.to/DragonTales
Writing Dark Stories http://myBook.to/WritingDark

The service is free to you, because the link shorteners earn a small commission from Amazon each time a click leads to a sale.

Try this one:
http://www.booklinker.net/

CHAPTER 24: GETTING PAST THE DREADED 2K HURDLE

When you follow 2,000 people, Twitter suddenly won't let you follow anyone else. You can no longer even followback people who follow you.

To remedy this, you need to get almost 2,000 people to follow you – a near impossibility if you can't follow people to entice them to followback.

At this stage, many Twitter users gnash their teeth, mutter curses against Twitter, and often give up altogether.

Don't. You can get past that barrier. I'll show you how.

THE METHOD

First, unfollow everyone who doesn't follow you back. This will take you away from the limit and give you room to manoeuvre. Then follow people who are likely to follow you in return.

Finding the people who don't follow you can be an arduous, tedious task, so use an app. Useful apps for this are ManageFlitter and Tweepi. The basic versions are free and all you need at this stage. Use them to show everyone whom you follow and who isn't following you, and to sort them by follow date. Unfollow the ones you've followed longest first, because they've had plenty of time to follow you if they wished.

Follow new people who are likely to follow you back. These are people who share your interests, are active Twitter users, who follow more people than they have followers, and who aren't themselves stuck at the 2K hurdle.

Other people's lists (see Chapter 11) and shoutouts (see Chapter 22) are useful sources.

Find my shoutout or list of 'Writers Who Followback Writers'. Currently, it contains 78 members who are committed to following you back if your profile describes you as a writer, author, novelist, poet, journalist or similar. If any don't honour their commitment, let me know, and I may remove them from the list.

If you're following me, tweet me (@RayneHall) to say you're stuck at the 2K hurdle. I may tweet a shoutout for you to my followers.

Ask your friends for shoutouts, too.

Tweeting *I need followers to get past the 2K hurdle. Can you help? (please retweet)* will probably bring several new followers. However, it will attract spam messages of the *Buy 10,000 followers cheap!* type. Ignore those.

WHAT NOT TO DO

Don't buy followers. Twitter spots those fakes quickly and deletes them, so you'll be back at the 2K hurdle.

ADVANCED STRATEGIES

To get past the 2K hurdle fast, temporarily adapt your Twitter strategies. For example, don't block anyone for a while. Instead, let anyone who likes follow you. You may even want to participate in some of the organised followback swaps. Look for hashtags like #teamfollowback. These yield followers who play the numbers game. Their tweets are likely to be uninteresting, and they won't read yours. You can unfollow them again later – but wait until you're well past the 2K hurdle, because if you unfollow them, they'll unfollow you.

OTHER LIMITS

Once you're past the 2K hurdle, everything becomes easier, and Twitter rarely restricts what you do.

You may still hit a limit, but it will be a short-term one. For example, Twitter limits how many people you may follow and how many tweets you may send per hour and per day. These limits vary from account to account, but are usually 1000 tweets and 1000 follows per day. If Twitter tells you that you have reached your follow or update limit, simply stop and continue the next day. Sometimes, waiting half an hour is enough and everything will be back to normal.

DO A GOOD DEED

Once you're past the 2K hurdle, follow some people (perhaps writer colleagues) who are still stuck.

CHAPTER 25: MANAGING A BUSY ACCOUNT

Once your account is thriving, when you follow many people, have many followers and tweet a lot, you'll look for ways to reduce the workload.

The choices you make at this stage determine whether your Twitter will be a success.

Many apps (services, programmes) promise to save you time, increase your popularity and make your use of Twitter more efficient.

However, what most of them do is ruin your platform faster than you built it.

Some are useful, and I'll discuss them in this and the following chapter.

WHAT NOT TO DO

Resist all temptation to 'automate' your Twitter. Automatic following, automatic greeting, automatic tweeting, automatic retweeting, automatic favouriting, automatic replies ... all these are driving your genuine audience away.

If you are already using automation services, turn them off now, before they damage your valuable platform further.

NOTIFICATIONS AND LISTS

When you follow many people, it's impossible to read every single person's every tweet. Trying to do this would drive you insane.

Compare it with real life, where you have thousands of acquaintances, but listen to only a few at a time. At certain times, you interact with colleagues, at others, with members of your family. Sometimes you converse with shop staff, members of the PTA or the church. The same applies to Twitter: pick one group of people whose tweets to read today, and a different group tomorrow.

Do this with lists. (See Chapter 11).

Another way to avoid overwhelming Twitter noise is not to read tweets in your timeline, where thousands rush past at high speed. Instead, click on 'Notifications' (or 'Interactions' as it is called in some places). Here you see tweets addressed to you, mentioning you, or replying to your tweets – in short, the important ones.

TWEETDECK

This is a safe and sensible app. Owned by Twitter, it is basically an extension of Twitter's standard service.

Although I find it a bit clunky to use and it is prone to crashing, it is invaluable for managing Twitter accounts, especially once you follow more than a thousand or so people.

Create columns. Each column is a mini-timeline, and you decide what appears in it. To start with, turn all your Twitter lists (see Chapter 11) into columns. You can set up additional columns, for example, for tweets containing certain hashtags such as #vampire or #amwriting. For each column, you have refinement options, e.g. to turn off retweets or to view tweets by people you follow only.

I often create temporary columns for specific projects I'm working on, and delete them when I'm done.

Unlike lists on Twitter, several TweetDeck columns can be viewed on a single page; no need to navigate from one to another.

If you have several Twitter accounts (see Chapter 14) you can manage them conveniently on TweetDeck without logging in and out all the time.

Tweetdeck also allows you to schedule tweets in advance, that is, to write a tweet now so that it will go out at a specified later time. However, other apps perform this service more smoothly. More about that in Chapter 26.

CHAPTER 26: SCHEDULING TWEETS

Here is another useful method to increase your tweeting efficiency – but consider carefully to what use you will put it. Applied thoughtlessly, it does more harm than good.

THE BASICS

You can write many tweets in advance, and schedule them to go out several hours or days apart.

This saves time, and it also keeps your account active and interesting when you have to be away from Twitter for a while.

Some apps allow bulk uploading of tweets, so you can write a hundred tweets at once, upload them, and re-use them at a later stage. Having certain tweets taken care of frees you to spend Twitter time interacting with your followers.

Most of these apps charge a subscription fee, but allow you to test the service free for a couple of weeks. The problem is that once your trial expires, you'll lose the work you've invested in setting things up.

Others have a free basic version and a fee-charging upgrade version. I suggest you try one of these, because you can keep using it whether or not you decide to upgrade.

WHAT NOT TO DO

With a scheduling app at your disposal, you may experience a near-irresistible temptation to upload masses of promo tweets and constantly send out the message *Buy my wonderful book* in many variations. Few users can resist the seductive lure.

Stay strong. Remember: the fewer promos you tweet, the more attention they get. Don't ruin your great platform now.

Some of these apps even write your tweets for you. You provide components, and the app assembles them in endless permutations, so that no two tweets are the same and Twitter won't notice and block the repetitions. But letting an app write your tweets is a definite no-no. Don't get lured by the convenience. Stay genuine.

ADVANCED STRATEGIES

Schedule your tweets for different times of the day. This way, they reach people all over the world who live in different time zones.

Create several groups of non-topical tweets of interest to your followers, and save each as a separate document. This allows you to switch from one type to another as required. For example, I have 'queues' for #writetip, #indiepubtip and #twittertip tweets, as well as for my shoutouts, writing memes and other cartoons.

When recycling a queue of promotional tweets, make sure the prices are still correct and the URLs are still appropriate. It is easy to commit blunders, for example, if you decide to give Amazon a three-month monopoly for your book via KDP Select, and continue to tweet the book's Nook and Smashwords links.

BUFFER

If you like an easy-to use scheduling app without frills, I suggest Buffer. The basic version is free, and is all you need as a light user. I rate Buffer's ease of use 10 out of 10. The helpfulness of the support staff (real people who want to solve your problems, not bots spewing automated answers) gets 10 out of 10 as well.

Another great feature of Buffer is that it facilitates easy sharing of websites. Whenever you come across a webpage that your followers might enjoy, click the Buffer button, and the URL to that site, complete with summary, gets scheduled as a tweet. I recommend that you edit these tweets, for example, by adding brief comments or hashtags. The webpage-sharing gets another 10/10 from me.

As an intense user, I have subscribed to the upgrade version which allows me to schedule a greater number of tweets, although the management of scheduled tweets with Buffer doesn't quite satisfy me and I would award it only 4 out of 10.

OTHER SCHEDULING APPS

If Buffer doesn't suit you, or you want to experiment further, browse the web for the searchword 'tweet scheduling app'. Beware, some are listed as 'free' but actually charge a fee, and some may be malware hosts tricking you into installing dangerous content on your computer.

I've sampled about a dozen apps, and still like Buffer best, despite its limitations.

For large-scale users (like myself), the queue management system of SocialOomph gets 10 out of 10 – but some of SocialOomph's other features are glitchy, clunky or damaging to your platform, e.g. by churning out automated DM and faked greetings, so I give them only 2 out of 10. As a long-term user, I rate SocialOomph's customer support 1/10.

Of course, these are just my personal opinions, and other people's experiences may differ.

MISTAKES I MADE AND LEARNT FROM

When I first discovered scheduling – with the HootSuite app – I got carried away and sent out as many scheduled tweets as Twitter permitted, flooding my followers with semi-automated messages.

After removing my books from Kobo (in protest against Kobo's abuse of indie authors), I uploaded a file of pre-written promo tweets about my books – forgetting that some of these tweets contained the Kobo URLs. I did not realise this until my followers alerted me that these links were dead.

CHAPTER 27: MEASURING SUCCESS

Apps can tell you how successful you are on Twitter – but take this information with a large pinch of salt.

HOW IT WORKS

Many apps measure your Twitter (or general social media) popularity, tell you which tweets are most successful, rate the usefulness of your strategies, highlight the topics you're influential in, rate your followers' engagement level, compare your standing with that of bestselling authors in your genre, identify your most influential followers, and more.

Many are free. Some are free for the basic version but charge you if you want in-depth information, others allow free use for a short trial period.

When you have a moment, check them out, and see what they say. You may find those insights interesting.

Try, for example
Klout.com, retweetrank.com, twitalyzer.com

But don't get lured into working to enhance your ratings, because the results are so ridiculously easy to manipulate that any improvement is meaningless.

If you want to increase your ratings, simply do this: create several Twitter accounts, and use them to retweet one another frequently. Your ratings will shoot up immediately. Participate in Twitter retweet cartels, and do some reciprocal voting with other users of the app. I did this for a while, and my alleged influence and popularity increased enormously – but it was all fake and therefore pointless.

A fun way to measure the hypothetical value of your Twitter account is Twalue.com. Try it for a chuckle, but don't take it seriously, because selling accounts is against Twitter's rules. Besides, the algorithm is based on quantities, and doesn't take quality into account. It also values users who follow few people higher than those who follow many, and gives higher credit to accounts that gain followers fast than to those that build their platform gradually – which in effect means the most 'valuable' accounts are those that have thousands of purchased fake followers. I consider this nonsense.

Twalue tells me that my Twitter is worth $36,957.05, which is interesting, though I believe the true value of my account – with the high ratio of genuine engaged followers, built over two years – would be much higher.

On a smaller scale, you can see how popular individual tweets are by checking how often they have been retweeted or favourited. You can see this information in Twitter or in TweetDeck immediately below the tweet. However, this data is flawed, because many of the retweets and favourites come from bots and automation apps, have no meaning and don't even indicate that the tweet has been read. Also, the counted retweets don't include the traditional style retweeting or modified retweets.

A more reliable indicator than retweets and favourites is the clickthrough rate which is the number of people who clicked on the link in your tweet to find out more. This is especially useful for promotional tweets about your book, with a link to the book's product page on Amazon, Barnes & Noble or Smashwords.

Clickthroughs show that your followers' interest has been tickled, and they chose to find out more about your book. Some of these clickthroughs will lead to downloads of the free sample pages, and a portion of those will hopefully lead to sales. When you compare the clickthrough rates of your promo tweets, you can see which of them has the best results.

Unfortunately, neither Twitter nor Tweetdeck show clickthroughs, but some apps do – including the free user-friendly app Buffer I recommend in Chapter 26.

WHAT NOT TO DO

Don't kid yourself that an increased ranking in a popularity-measuring app signifies genuine popularity.

Don't waste time manipulating the results of such apps. It's easy to do, meaningless, and it won't enhance your brand or your book sales. I doubt that anyone thinks 'I fancy reading this thriller. I must log into Klout and see the author's Klout ranking before I decide'.

Be sceptical when you read that people with high ratings in a certain app receive better service in hotels, improved aeroplane seating, speedier customer service and more lucrative job offers. When you track these stories to their source, you may find they were written by the app's publicists.

MISTAKES I MADE AND LEARNT FROM

For several months, I worked to improve my ranking and subject list at Klout, which measures how influential people are. Annoyed that Klout ranked me as an expert on subjects in which I had no interest (such as Boston Red Sox, Nook and Pizza) I was determined to set the record straight. Getting ranked high for the right topics (writing, publishing, horror etc) became almost an obsession. I swapped K+ credits with other Klout members, confirming that they had influenced me in the topics of their choice. I used my own duplicate accounts (@SuzieScrybe, @FrancoFolly et al) to award further K+, and enlisted the help of other Twitter-using writers.

Sure, my Klout ranking shot up, and the topic list became more appropriate. But did this actually increase my influence? Nope – not one bit. Did it enhance my Twitter account? Did it get me known? Did it sell my books? Not at all.

When I realised how much time I was spending on Klout – hundreds of hours which would have been better applied to tweeting or writing – I stopped.

For a short time, I also aimed to get into the top 5% of most retweeted people worldwide at RetweetRank. That was the phase when I engaged in mass retweet swaps. My ranking did indeed increase, but only by fractions of percent.

Eventually I realised that the ranking mattered nothing, and that retweets are meaningless unless they get read, so I ceased. Instead, I focused on producing tweets that people would actually read. Interestingly, I'm now in the top 2% of most retweeted people worldwide - and it's a genuine, un-manipulated result.

CHAPTER 28: APPS, APPS AND MORE APPS

Many programmes exist that make (or claim to make) Twitter more effective. They are referred to as 'Twitter apps' (app = short for 'application'). As writers, we don't need any of them, though some can be useful.

I've already discussed scheduling apps (mostly useful) and success-measuring apps (mostly a time sink).

TWEET MANAGEMENT

This overlaps with scheduling. Write tweets in advance, schedule them to go out at different times, and re-use them. This can be a valid part of a Twitter strategy.

However, tweet management apps also offer functions you may want to avoid, for example:
- Writing your tweets for you by combining phrases you provide in endless permutations
- Automated 'Thanks for following me' tweets and DMsq
- Automated responses to keywords (e.g. whenever someone mentions 'vampire', the app sends a reply in your name, advertising your vampire novel)
- Automated retweeting of tweets with certain keywords or by certain people

FOLLOWER MANAGEMENT

Sometimes it's helpful to sort your followers, for example, you may want to see all followers with the word 'vampire' in their profile, or those whose recent tweets include the hashtag #amwriting. Twitter doesn't provide this feature, but some apps do.

Unfortunately, most services provided by follower management apps do more harm than good. For example, they promise to weed out spammers and fake accounts. This is ridiculous, since we want to weed those out from the accounts we follow; the ones who follow us don't matter in this respect.

Worse, some apps offer to 'clean up' your Twitter followers. They select accounts their algorithms consider bad, and use 'force unfollow'. 'Force unfollow' simply means 'block', so many of the followers who used to receive and enjoy your tweets, suddenly find themselves blocked by you. Blocking is an aggressive action, and some people feel greatly hurt when it happens to them.

The criteria these apps apply to identify 'bad' accounts are hair-raising.

For example, they purge 'inactive' accounts – these are people who haven't tweeted for a while. But the fact that they don't tweet much themselves doesn't mean that they don't read tweets. These may be shy, quiet people who simply like to read rather than talk – and they may be the very people who adore your books! They may be happy to read what their favourite author has to say, and suddenly they find that this author has blocked them. You can imagine how this makes them feel. It's a sure way to lose fans fast.

The follower management apps also purge accounts that tweet excessively, and block those from following you as well. 'Excessive' tweeting includes everyone who chats a lot with others – i.e. real people who engage on Twitter, exactly the kind of follower you want.

Even if you don't like people who tweet all the time, it's for you to unfollow them. Blocking them from following you is pointless.

If you use a follower management app at all, I urge you to review every single account before you delete it. Don't let it do any 'purging', 'clean-up' and 'force-unfollow' in one fell swoop.

Personally, I've decided that follower management is of no use to me.

FOLLOWING MANAGEMENT

This is potentially useful to unfollow people who aren't following you back. To me, Twitter is a two-way communication, and I unfollow people who treat me as a passive recipient of their one-way broadcasts. From time to time, I use an app to unfollow the people who aren't following me back.

ManageFlitter (the free basic version) is a useful app for this, especially if you have hit the dreaded 2K hurdle. Use it (or another app) to show everyone whom you follow and who isn't following you back. Sort them in follow order – so the ones whom you've followed for the longest time show up first. If they haven't followed you back for a month or more, they're not going to. Unfollow them.

You can also organise your reciprocal following this way. Call up everyone who follows you and whom you are not following back yet. However, you may need some self-discipline to resist the temptation to 'select all' and follow everyone back. Many of these are automated accounts that follow people randomly in the expectation that some will follow back. They have no interest in reading your tweets. A large number are spam accounts and other undesirables.

When creating a page of everyone who follows you and whom you're not following back yet, select to see their profile text. This will show whether these people share your interests and may be interesting conversation partners, or whether they have followed you at random.

Remember: **Your Twitter power lies in choosing whom to follow. Don't surrender this to an app.**

Apps also identify people whom you may want to follow, mostly by looking for keywords in profiles and tweets. This sounds like a useful feature, but in practice, you can do this yourself with Twitter's or TweetDeck's search function.

Some apps do the actual following for you. Be careful – this is against Twitter's rules.

INFORMATION-GATHERING

Some apps provide information about your followers – their habits, preferences, tweet times and more. You can call up statistics of what percentage of followers lives in which country or which city, what their education level and average annual income is, and more. Some of this is mind-boggling.

This kind of data can give you a tremendous advantage when planning a marketing campaign. However, it does not come cheap. These apps charge hefty subscription fees. Although they often offer free basic versions, those seldom reveal anything useful other than what you already know – such as how many followers you have.

One app – which shall remain nameless – lured me with promises of certain kinds of data free. I spent a lot of time filling in the required forms – only to be informed that this data is available only with the (expensive) 'professional' version.

Another (expensive) app provided a vast range of insights into my followers: what newspapers they read, what their favourite clothing brands are, even how many of them purchased books from Barnes & Noble. The latter whetted my appetite. An app that could tell me what proportion of my followers shopped at Barnes & Noble versus Amazon was worth a subscription! However, Amazon was not mentioned. No bookseller was, other than Barnes & Noble, which made the information useless to me. When I queried this, staff told me they didn't include Amazon because it wasn't a real shop, only an online company. Ahem. I decided against subscribing.

FAKE FOLLOWER CHECKERS

Some apps purport to reveal how many fake followers you (and other people) have. At first, this seemed a cool app. I was glad to see I had zero fakes.

Whenever an author had far more followers than they were following, I ran their user name through the app, and very often, it was revealed that their many followers were fakes. Far from being popular, they were paying money for fake followers.

However, some of my Twitter friends also had a high ratio of fakes, and this startled me. I didn't think they were desperate and stupid enough to do this. Had I misjudged them?

Then a British politician was accused of faking it. Her opponents used the app's result to 'prove' that she was cheating. She maintained her innocence, claiming she had no idea where the fakes came from.

Soon, it became a favourite tactic of election campaigners to expose the number of fake accounts following the opposing candidate, using the app-provided results as 'evidence'.

At this stage, I grew suspicious – not of the politicians, but of the apps. I did a simple test. I chose people who I'm sure would not bother to buy fakes, and I ran their user names through the apps. The result? Almost all of them – including @DalaiLama – allegedly use fake followers to pretend they're popular.

So don't rely on the results of those apps. They may be more fake than the people they claim to expose.

TWEET-LENGTHENING

Sometimes, 140 characters just isn't enough to say what you mean. Here's an app that allows you to extend your tweet: www.twitlonger.com.

Be careful not to use it much, though. Your followers may feel you're cheating if you don't stick to the prescribed character limit, which is the spirit of Twitter and half the fun. You may also come across as someone who isn't able to write tight – not a good image for an author.

Another consideration is that to see the full message, people need to click. Most people don't click URLs unless they're interested – and if you haven't managed to hook them with the first few words, they won't bother to read the rest.

However, the tweet-lengthening service has its uses, perhaps in conversations, or to present factual information.

GRANTING PERMISSION TO APPS TO USE YOUR TWITTER ACCOUNT

Typically, when you use an app, you either create an account with them, or you can simply access them with your Twitter account. Either way the app needs permission to use your Twitter.
You will see a screen message that shows what the app will and won't be allowed to do. Check this carefully. 'See your password' should be among the 'not allowed' items.

Most apps demand the right to send tweets from your account. Don't be alarmed by this. It doesn't mean that the app will, only that you can choose to send tweets directly from the app. However, certain apps take advantage. They use your account to send tweets advertising their own service.

Some send a tweet whenever you use their service, others automatically send a tweet once a week or once a day.

These automated advertising tweets typically look like this:

Contributed tweets are provided by [nuisance app's name]
I have automated my Twitter. Why don't you? [nuisance app's URL]
Save time! Gain new followers! Use [nuisance app's name], it's great!!!
Today, X number people followed me, Y number unfollowed. Statistics provided by [nuisance app's name]

Such auto-tweets signal that your Twitter actions are (at least in part) faked. It's a quick way to lose your followers' trust and respect.

Some apps actually send insulting tweets in your name. A while back, a certain nuisance app generated this tweet: *I've caught X number sneaky unfollowers!*

Are people 'sneaky' if they exercise the freedom to unfollow who they please? What does this say about the person who (supposedly) sent this? As you can imagine, this tweet roused a lot anger – and the alleged senders were unaware they had sent it! The app was tweeting it without their knowledge.

Unfortunately, many apps presume the right to send junk in your name by default, but most of them allow you to change it. Go to the app's 'Settings' tab. There should be an option to disable such tweets.

Some will not allow you to opt out of this unless you pay a fee. In my opinion, that's nasty. I would stay clear of any app that demands payment to stop tweeting junk from my account.

I prefer apps which don't tweet anything unless I choose it. Some unlock additional benefits each time we tweet about them, and they leave it to us to decide. I think that's fair.

If an app turns out to do more harm than good, leave it at once – even if you've paid a subscription. Cut your losses and protect your account, your platform and your reputation. The quickest and surest way to stop an app from using your account is to revoke its access.

Go to your Twitter account, click the cogwheel icon, click 'Settings', click 'Apps'. Now you see all the apps to which you have granted permission to use your account. These may be more than you think. Consider which ones you want to keep. For the others, click 'Revoke   Access'.

CHAPTER 29: INTERACTING WITH FANS

If you're an unpublished writer, you can skip this chapter. For published authors, this chapter is essential.

The most important tweets you'll get are those in which fans tell you they love your book. Cherish them.

THE BASICS

When someone tweets you to say they've bought your book, that they've started or finished reading, and that they enjoyed it, reply!

If possible, phrase your response as a question. Here are some examples:

When they just bought the book: *Enjoy! Did you download the free sample first?*
When they've just started reading: *What do you think of it so far?*
For novels: *Do you think [character name] has made the right choice?*
Who is your favourite character?
For anthologies and collections: *Which of the stories is your personal favourite?*
For non-fiction books: *Which chapter did you find most helpful for your [home/business/dog/whatever]?*

This gives five instant benefits:
1. It makes the reader feel valued.
2. It gives you insights into what your readers like.
3. It creates 'customer loyalty' (that is, it makes it likely that the reader will buy another book by you).

4. It stimulates word-of-mouth (makes it more likely that the reader will mention this book to friends).
5. It creates interaction on Twitter (always a good thing).
6. Other people can see the nice things the reader is saying about your book.

To encourage readers to tweet you, put your user name in a 'Dear Reader' section at the end of the book. You may also offer to follow them back if they tweet you and say they've read your book.

When fans tweet to say they enjoyed your book, treat them as testimonials – the kind of genuine testimonial marketing professionals dream about and that money can't buy. Favourite and retweet those tweets. This shows the fan that you value their communication, and it promotes your book in a more trust-inspiring way than if you said those things yourself.

Create a private Twitter list and a TweetDeck column for fans. This list will be your most precious Twitter asset. Use it to keep in touch with your fans, and do it wisely. Read what they tweet, and respond to it. You may want to make this a regular event, perhaps once a week. This is the best investment you can make of your Twitter time. Resist the temptation to address promo tweets to individual fans – you would lose their loyalty fast.

WHAT NOT TO DO

When a fan tells you they loved your book, don't respond with a promotion.

Bad response:
Glad you enjoyed 'The Vamp Vanishes'. My second book 'The Vanished Vamp Returns' is even better! Buy it here: www....

That would be a big turn off, and almost certainly stop them from buying any book of yours again.

Negative and nasty tweets about your books are rare. If you get one, don't argue with the reader, and don't try to change their opinion. Either ignore it (if it's nasty) or reply politely (if the reader simply didn't like the book). Here's how you can phrase your reply:

@readersname *Interesting. Thanks for sharing your opinion.*

Don't favourite these tweets, or include the senders in your list of fans. They won't buy your next book anyway. Tastes differ, and you can't please everyone.

ADVANCED STRATEGIES

When a reader tweets you that they enjoyed your book, invite them to review it. This is the best kind of review you can possibly get: genuine, authentic, personal, positive.

I like to do this after I've asked a question about their reading experience (*How do you feel about Dahoud? Do you want to hug him or castrate him?*) and received a reply.

Make sure you don't come across as pushy or demanding. Here's how I phrase it:

Would you consider writing a review of this book on Amazon or Barnes & Noble?

Very often, they feel honoured to be asked, and happy to do us this favour.

To see fan tweets about your books which are not addressed to you, search your pen name. I recommend doing this with TweetDeck rather than Twitter, and to create a column that shows all tweets containing your name. Not all will be about you and your book (I get tweets about events in the village hall in Rayne, England) but most will be.

Do the same for the titles of your books. This way, you can see the word-of-mouth recommendations. (*I'm reading an awesome vampire story by Suzie Scrybe* or *My puppy used to do the same – it drove me nuts! There's a book that really helped, called The Zen of Dog Training or s/th like that.*)

Favourite and retweet them, and if appropriate, reply.

"The followers who like my tweets matter more to me than those who don't. Those are welcome to simply unfollow."

- Rayne Hall

MISTAKES I MADE AND LEARNT FROM

At the end of my books, I invite people to tweet me, and I promise to follow them back. I do this faithfully – but I worry that I missed some during the time when I didn't have internet access. I hope they'll forgive me. (If you read this, and I'm not following you back yet, prod me.)

I wish I had collected fans in a list from the start, so I could interact with them specifically and maybe do them little favours sometimes. But I started only a year ago, and I haven't even been conscientious about it. Often, I responded to fan tweets, but forgot to click 'Add to List'. I really need to become more organised about this.

CHAPTER 30: STAYING SAFE

Everything you do online brings risks. With Twitter, it is relatively easy to avoid the main dangers. Here is how.

LINKS

Don't click any links unless you know where they lead. Often, the URL itself contains this information. For example, it contains the word 'Smashwords' or 'iTunes'. BookShow.Me and Viewbook.At links lead to Amazon. Links to blog posts and news articles are also usually safe.

However, be on your guard when you receive a tweet addressed to you individually, which seems to be personal.
Is this what you mean?
Haha. Is this you in the photo?
This person is spreading nasty rumours about you.
Have you seen what your ex says about you?
I can't believe the nasty things about you. This is so mean.

This type of tweet is designed to elicit your trust and make you so curious or angry that you will set caution aside and click the link. Don't.

The link leads to a site infected with malware, and by clicking you enable the hackers to hijack your account. Now they can send the same tweets from your account, without you even realising.

Most often, these tweets are sent by Direct Message (DM). Be very suspicious of any link you get by DM.

Even if the tweet's sender is a friend, their account may have been hacked. Ask your friend if they really sent this before you click.

When you receive such a tweet, don't block the sender or report them for spam. They are innocent victims of a hacking attack. Instead, go to their profile and see if their account sends similar tweets to other people. Alert them, perhaps with a tweet like this:

@SuzieScrybe It looks like your account has been hacked. It sends malware tweets.

If you have already clicked such a link, check if your account is sending tweets without your knowledge. If yes, change your password immediately. This usually puts a stop to the problem.

PASSWORDS

Choose a long password, mixing uppercase and lowercase letters, and inserting some numbers and punctuation. Don't use any words from your profile information, such as the title of your book, because those are easy to guess.

Don't make it the same password you use for other social media sites, for shopping or banking. In case one account gets hacked, you want to prevent the hackers from accessing the others.

Change your password several times a year.

If you need to share your password with someone – perhaps you've hired a virtual assistant or engaged the services of a social media marketer – use one you don't use anywhere else, and change it as soon as their job is done.

PERSONAL INFORMATION

Unlike some other social media, Twitter doesn't display personal data such as your birthday, the town of your birth, who you're married to, and your mother's maiden name. This makes it less likely that confidence tricksters will mine your Twitter information to impersonate you.

However, take care not to reveal too much about yourself. Avoid mentioning your birthday, the town of your birth, your mother's maiden name and such in tweets. Definitely don't put them into the profile text where everyone can access it at a glance.

Also consider your – and your family's - safety outside the internet. Don't share your postal or email address. Think twice before you reveal the names and ages of your children and what swimming pool they visit every Tuesday afternoon.

If you want to give personal information to an individual, send them a tweet like this:

@SuzieScrybe I'm going to send you a DM in a moment.

Then send the Direct Message with the confidential information. This way, only the recipient receives it.

PROTECTED TWEETS

If you like, you can make your tweets 'protected' instead of 'public'. This way, only approved followers can see them. I think this is not a good choice. People may not follow you unless they see what you tweet, so you're losing out on real followers, and you also miss the opportunity to gain attention with your tweets and attract new fans.

What's the advantage of not making your tweets visible? For people like you and me, I see none. Frankly, if you don't want your messages to be seen, don't tweet them.

WHAT NOT TO DO

If you change your password because the account has been hacked, you may receive an email asking you to reconfirm the new password. Caution: although this request appears to come from Twitter, it's from the hackers who want to know your password so they can continue using your account. Don't tell them.

Some services offer free features, but require you to share your password. For example, they promise 10,000 new followers or an in-depth analysis of your Twitter account. Don't take the bait. They plan to use your account for their own purposes – to follow people you have no interest in, to lend authenticity to their fake accounts, to tweet promotions and to spam.

CHAPTER 31: HOW TO SPOT FAKES

A large portion of Twitter accounts are fakes. Some are total fakes (mass-generated by spam companies), others are semi-automated by people who are too lazy to interact and tweet but expect others to read their tweets. The former are best avoided, the latter may or may not be worth following.

SIGNS OF A FAKE ACCOUNT

Here are the red flags to watch out for. They do not necessarily mean these aren't real people, but if several apply, chances are it's a fake.

* No profile picture. Instead, it shows the blank 'egghead'. This is often the case when spam companies create thousands of new accounts. However, it may also be a Twitter newbie who hasn't yet uploaded a picture.

* Implausibly glamorous profile picture. These are stock photos of professional models. The account is usually a spam bot, typically one that sells pornographic services. (Twitter cracks down on porn peddlers, but they resurface frequently.) However, it may also be a teenager with self-esteem issues.

* No profile text. The companies that create fake accounts by the thousands often don't take time to write biographical information. However, it might be someone who is shy or who doesn't know how social media work.

* Profile text is a quote or aphorism. Spam companies know that profiles without text don't invite trust, so they fill in the texts with quotes of famous people and witty sayings. Real people seldom do that – they may tweet their favourite quotes, but don't use them as profile texts. Of course, there are exceptions.

* Far more retweets than original tweets. When you visit their profile, you may see a whole page of retweets and nothing else.

* Their account sends automated advertising for the apps they use, for example:
Contributed tweets are by [name of app]
Today's statistics provided by [name of app]: x number followers, y number unfollowers.
I'm saving time by using [name of app]. It's great! Try it! [URL of app]
Accounts sending such tweets are at least semi-automated. The real person may appear occasionally.

* As soon as you follow, you receive a DM of this type:
Thanks for following me. Please like my Facebook/visit my blog/buy my product.
Thanks for the follow. You've made my day!
These are almost always auto-generated with apps.

Some sophisticated apps even pick up information from your profile and weave it into the automated DM message. For example, if your profile says 'author' they'll write: *Thanks for following. Your book looks interesting, I'll check it out.* or *Thanks for following. I love your book cover.*

The results can be positively creepy. I remember when I was new to Twitter and received a DM that said *Thanks for following. I'll seek you out next time I'm in Sussex.* I didn't cherish the prospect of getting stalked by a stranger.

If you get an auto-DM, it may be from a fake account, or it may be from a real person who is faking their Twitter presence. If someone's immediate response to a new follower is an automated reply faking the personal touch, chances are most of their tweets are automated too, and not worth reading. Some people hit 'unfollow' immediately when they get an automated greeting, but you may not want to go that far.

CONVERSATION FAKERS

Some bots (short for robots, i.e. automated accounts) are programmed to jump into ongoing conversations and dump their spam message.

Others reply to random tweets, pretending to pick up a conversation thread, but really just inserting a spam link.
@SuzieScrybe. I agree! So glad you said this. Here's something you should see http//...

Many spam bots are programmed to respond to certain keywords or phrases. For example, when someone tweets about needing more followers, the bots will reply with

@SuzieScrybe Here's how to get 601 new followers in one day!

If you mention 'real estate' and 'California' in the same tweet, you may get automated replies trying to sell you Californian property.

Most of these automated conversation-fakers are not cleverly programmed, and you can see through them quickly. However, some are sophisticated. It may take a while before you realise you're chatting with a bot.

I imagine there are probably many bots talking with bots on Twitter, trying to sell each other stuff.

WHAT NOT TO DO

Don't become one of those conversation fakers. Stay away from any app that offers auto-response, auto-greet, auto-retweet, auto-anything.

Don't send 'thanks for following' messages, or you may be mistaken for a bot. If you want to show your appreciation, read your new follower's recent tweets, and reply to one of them. This will be appreciated.

MISTAKES I MADE AND LEARNT FROM

During my first months on Twitter, I received many tweets *Thanks for following. I love your book cover.* Since I had more than forty books published, I always tweeted back, *Which cover do you mean?* It took me a while to realise that these tweets were automated, created by apps which picked up the word 'author' from my profile.

CHAPTER 32: CELEBRITIES AND INFLUENCERS

On Twitter, you will meet many famous and important people. You can follow them if you wish, and maybe some of them will follow you back.

CELEBRITIES

Rock stars, Hollywood actors, religious leaders, political rulers and bestselling authors use Twitter, and you can read their tweets. However, many accounts held in their names are actually managed by fans – with or without the VIP's consent.

To make sure you're following the real person, go to the account which has a little blue symbol with a tick behind the name. This shows that Twitter has verified this account: it really is that famous person.

Be aware that many celebrities don't manage their own accounts or even write their own tweets. They hire a social media manager who does this for them. Those accounts tend to be dull, often just endless promos and pictures of the celebrity at events.

Remarkably, most famous writers' tweets seem to be genuine and are usually entertaining, perhaps because these people enjoy writing and are good at it.

You may find their tweets entertaining and inspiring. You can also observe how they use Twitter, and perhaps learn from them. Here are some blue-tick authors you may want to follow:

@StephenKing, @jk_rowling, @neilhimself (that's Neil Gaiman), @AnneRiceAuthor, @benmezrich, @MargaretAtwood, @jodipicoult, @BenHatch @LisaGardnerBks, @tessgerritsen

INFLUENCERS

An 'influencer' is someone who has the power to persuade others. They are experts in their fields, are active in the social media, have many followers, and importantly, their followers listen to them.

Some of the influencers, but not all, are also celebrities.

Marketing and public relations professionals court social media influencers the way they once courted journalists. If they can get an influencer to say something nice about their product on Twitter, this recommendation counts for a lot.

There are many apps that will identify the influencers in your field with various degrees of accuracy. Some calculate the level of influence based on the number of followers and retweets – which has little to do with real influence if the followers are automated accounts and the retweets are automated. Others factor in more useful indicators, such as how much engagement they receive.

You may not need an app to tell you who the influencers in your field are. Franco Folly, author of dog training manuals, probably knows who the leading influencers in the field of dog training are, because he has been influenced by them. You can probably tell who has influenced you in the field you're writing about.

The funny thing is, I'm an 'influencer'. I have many followers, and I receive many retweets and a lot of engagement. When you use an app to determine who the most influential Twitter users are in the fields of writing, horror, book publishing, indie publishing etc, my name may crop up.

Because I'm an influencer, a lot of people (especially marketing and PR professionals) want my attention. They follow me, retweet me, contact me. This started very suddenly about six months ago when my name first registered in certain apps among the 'most influential' people.

They reckon that if they retweet my book promotion tweets, I will retweet their product promos in return – but unless their tweets are of interest to my followers, I won't.

Influencers are worth cultivating, but only those with genuine influence, and only those in your field.

HOW TO GET CELEBRITIES AND INFLUENCERS TO FOLLOW YOU

Apparently, to get important people to follow you, you simply need to be an influencer yourself.

As soon as I reached influencer status, blue-tick celebrities and major influencers started to follow me. Currently, I have about fifty followers with blue ticks.

The interesting thing is, most of these celebrities are from different fields, and we have nothing in common. I don't flatter myself that they read my tweets. Rather, their social media managers identified me as an 'influencer' and followed me, so that I would follow them back, and hopefully retweet their tweets.

I do follow them back – how can I resist a reciprocal arrangement with a film star? - but I don't retweet their messages unless they say something which my followers will like.

Interestingly, some influencers and celebrities (or rather, their social media managers) use dirty hit-and-run follow techniques. They follow many people, and as soon as we follow them back, they unfollow us, expecting us to be too awed to unfollow them, too. Well, I have no reluctance to hit 'unfollow' for famous people.

If you want celebrity followers, use an app such as Tweepi to identify 'verified' accounts, and sort them by followers:following ratio. Choose those who follow almost as many people as they have followers. Their strategy is to follow almost everyone, so they will probably follow you. However, don't count on them reading your tweets.

If you can engage an influencer in a conversation, great. But expect to be ignored by most. Try the ones who are well-known only in your field. They are most likely to respond, the exchange will be most interesting, and any resulting benefits (new followers, free publicity) will be targeted and therefore useful.

ADVANCED STRATEGIES

Instead of following celebrities (who almost certainly won't follow you back), add them to a Twitter list or a TweetDeck column. This allows you to read their tweets without following them.

CHAPTER 33: TWITTER FOR INTROVERTS

Social media are ideal tools for introverts who want to socialise yet stay fully in control of where, when, and with how much noise. Nobody knows how terrified you feel, and you can safely withdraw at any time without awkwardness. Twitter may be the best social network for people like us. If the noise and activity get overwhelming sometimes, here are some techniques.

Who are the people you want to reach on Twitter? Probably readers or writers, or both. People who love the written word are often introverts like us, and even those who're not introvert themselves, appreciate thoughtful depth, privacy and quiet interactions. This means these are people with whom you can be comfortable. Seek out like-minded people by searching for profiles with 'bookworm', 'writer' or similar.

Ignore the noisy, hectic, quarrel-seeking types. They're not your target audience anyway.

I have started to compile a Twitter list of 'Introvert Writers', to facilitate this kind of networking. If you follow those people and interact with them, their style may be a good match with yours. The list is still small, but growing. If you tweet me that you're an introvert writer, I'll add you to the list. This may bring you more followers of the kind you appreciate.

I'm proud to be an introvert. Most of the best writers are.

— Rayne Hall

Twitter gives you great control over who you want to listen to, how and when you want to interact. Use this power. If anyone annoys you or causes you stress, simply unfollow them, and if they persist, block them. Visit Twitter when you feel like it, for as long as you want. When you've had enough, just stop. The tweets will still be there for you to read later if you wish.

Social networks allow us to socialise from the privacy of our home with no need to join nosy parties and get jostled in crowded rooms. Unlike some other social networks, Twitter doesn't feature flashing pop-ups and blaring noises to force our attention. We can read tweets in silence. I really appreciate this.

'Notifications' can be annoying. Twitter sends an email or text message whenever something happens on your account, for example whenever someone retweets, and even when someone retweets a retweet. On top of that, Twitter sends a Notification each time it wants to advertise something. These bothersome Notifications intrude into our email boxes or mobile phones and can be a never-ending nuisance.

For peace and quiet, simply turn the Notifications off. Click the cogwheel icon at the top of the page. Click 'settings'. Click 'email Notifications'. Now you see a long list of options for everything Twitter wants to notify you about. I suggest you de-select every one.

Unfortunately, Twitter frequently introduces new options, and assumes by default that we agree to be notified. So even though we opted out of everything, suddenly the bothersome Notifications start again, and they continue until we de-select the latest nuisance. This is one of my major gripes about Twitter. I've turned off all email from Twitter. Click the cogwheel, click 'settings', click 'email Notifications', go to 'email is enabled', click 'turn off'.

CHAPTER 34: WEIRD REASONS WHY PEOPLE UNFOLLOWED ME ON TWITTER

More than 50,000 people follow me on Twitter @RayneHall... and every day, several unfollow me. Some even tell me why. Here's a selection of their reasons:

1. Tweets in inferior English (British).
2. I laughed at their jokes.
3. I did not laugh at their jokes.
4. I didn't buy their book.
5. Stalking (I followed them).
6. Plagiarism (I retweeted their tweet).
7. Failure to reply to their question within 16 minutes.
8. They saw no tweets but mine in their timeline (they weren't actually following anyone else).
9. I had more followers than they.
10. Horses get killed in one of my books.
11. I tweeted more about my own books than about theirs.
12. They always follow and unfollow the same people as their mates.
13. Not enough commas in my tweets.
14. I declined to read their unpublished novel.
15. I declined to retweet their poetry.
16. I declined to change my tweeting style to suit their personal taste.
17. I declined to fund their Kickstarter project.
18. By posting #writetip tweets I implied that the person's writing needed improvement (insult).
19. Too many tweets about writing and publishing.

20. My chats with other people appeared in their timeline.

21. I'm an insufferable prude. (I objected to close-up photos of genitalia).

22. I chatted more with other people than with them.

23. After chatting with me, they suddenly got new followers. They didn't like that.

24. Rayne Hall is not a real person, but a bot. Everyone knows that.

"If you don't like my tweets, simply unfollow me."
— Rayne Hall

Of course, these are only the ones who gave their reasons. (*Your use of British English disgusts me! Learn proper English before you tweet!! I unfollow!!!!*) Others didn't allow me a glimpse into their motivations. Who knows? Even weirder reasons may lurk in their minds.

CHAPTER 35: TEN SIGNS YOU'RE ADDICTED TO TWITTER

1. You check your Twitter every morning before breakfast, before brushing your teeth, before anything.
2. You frequently visit Twitter for a quick look, and before you know, you've spent an hour reading and writing tweets.
3. You catch yourself using hashtags in your emails and book manuscripts.
4. You have more Twitter followers than real-life acquaintances.
5. When someone annoys you in real life, you look for the 'block' button.
6. When something interesting happens, you immediately wonder how to describe it in under 140 characters.
8. You check daily how many people have followed, unfollowed, retweeted and favourited you.
9. You tweet from your mobile as you walk.
10. The thought of more than one day without Twitter access brings out cold sweat.

CHAPTER 36: FREQUENTLY ASKED QUESTIONS

Here are questions I get asked a lot by my followers. My answers are personal and true for myself. They're not meant to be rules about how others should use their Twitter accounts.

You follow over 40,000 people. Do you really read all their tweets?

Of course not. That would amount to several tweets per second, twenty-four hours a day. I select what kind of tweets I want to read and when. One day, I may read tweets by the authors whose stories I published in the *Ten Tales* books. Another day, it's fans of my books or people I've had nice chats with in the past. I use Twitter lists and TweetDeck columns for this (see Chapters 11 and 25). Now and then, I glance at the general timeline. Most of what appears there is just uninteresting promo noise, but sometimes a genuine tweet appears and I may respond to that.

How much time do you spend on Twitter every day?

This varies greatly. Some days, it's only five minutes. Others, it may be several hours. I've never measured it. Probably, I spend too much – especially when I should do other things, such as clean the bathroom or write a chapter.

Can I really build an account like yours in just two years?

I see no reason why you shouldn't, if you're willing to put the effort into it. You'll probably achieve it faster, because you can learn from my mistakes and avoid the errors that wasted much of my time.

I see you tweet at all times of the day. Do you ever sleep?

Sometimes I wake up in the middle of the night, and then I do some tweeting before I go back to sleep. I also type some tweets in advance and schedule them to go out several hours apart, so they reach people who live in different time zones. (See Chapter 26.)

What do you have against automation? I simply want to create some buzz for my book. I don't have time to read tweets and interact and do all the things you recommend.

Reality check: you don't have the time to read other people's tweets – but you expect them to read yours? Sorry to burst your bubble, but your automated promo tweets won't create a buzz for your book.

How often should I tweet? Is there an ideal number of tweets per day?

Tweet as much as you like. It's not the quantity of tweets, but the quality that counts. Some people claim that 4 (or 7 or 25) tweets per day is most effective, but I find that's nonsense. Some of your followers want to hear from you often, others only now and then. There's no way you can get it exactly right for everyone anyway, so just go ahead and have fun. Personally, I choose to tweet a lot, and most (not all) of my followers like it.

Has Twitter changed much since you joined?

Oh yes. Several changes were by Twitter itself – new layouts, new features, even new rules. Auto-followback is forbidden now, but when I started, Twitter actually encouraged its use! I'm glad to say I realised how stupid auto-followback was before Twitter did.

The overall use of Twitter has changed. There's much more automation and promotion going on now with fake accounts, auto-retweeting and such on an ever-larger scale. However, the same development happened everywhere on the internet, not just on Twitter. Genuine Twitter users have learnt to simply ignore all the automated crap.

Two years ago, tweets with inspiring quotes by famous people were popular and got retweeted a lot. Now, there are so many of them that they get largely ignored.

Twitter has become more visual, and the current trend is to use pictures to attract attention and entertain followers.

Why don't you show screenshots in this book?

The view is different, depending on what kind of device you use. On your iPod, it looks different than on your PC. Also, Twitter often changes the layout.

What do you think of 'promoted tweets'? Do you promote yours?

I ignore promoted tweets, and I don't pay to promote mine. I want people to read my tweets because they want to read them, not because Twitter rams my tweets down their throats.

I hate seeing 'promoted tweets' in my timeline, from people whom I don't follow. How do I stop this advertising?

Simply ignore it. Twitter, like any other social network, needs to make money. So far, I find advertising on Twitter far less intrusive than elsewhere. I read my tweets in Connections and in TweetDeck, where the paid-for advertising tweets don't appear – although I fear it's only a matter of time before advertising invades there, too.

If a particular promoted tweet raises your hackles, you can elect not to receive that kind of advert again. Do this repeatedly, and after a while, you'll see only tolerable adverts, and perhaps even some that you like. That's in the interest of everyone.

But I find it easiest to just ignore promoted tweets.

Where can I report cyber bullying, trolls and abuse tweets?

Twitter doesn't police content. Instead it's up to us to unfollow (or block) people whose tweets offend us.

Sadly, this means there's a lot of religious and racial hate-mongery going on, and cyber bullies can hound vulnerable victims without fear of repercussions.

At the time of writing, there's no easy reporting system in place for reporting trolls and cyber bullies and people who incite racial hatred and sexual violence. I wish there were. I witnessed cyber bullies (or maybe just one troll with several accounts) haranguing a helpless young girl driving her to despair, and when I tried to report it, Twitter simply didn't want to know.

The reason is that most offences are personal, and Twitter doesn't want to get involved in private quarrels.

So we're on our own. It's up to each individual to take responsibility for what happens within our own Twitter sphere. Use 'unfollow' when someone's tweets displease you, and 'block' if they attack you personally. Above all, be careful about what you retweet, so you don't unwittingly help racist hate-mongers and bullying trolls.

Update: Just as this book is about to be published, Twitter has added a reporting feature at last. Go to the user's profile, click 'Block or Report', click 'This user is abusive' and fill in the form.

Someone has blocked me, what should I do?

Nothing. If they don't want you to read their tweets, that's their choice. Their tweets may not be worth reading anyway.

It's possible that they blocked you by accident, or by naively using one of those apps that 'clean up' followers. If it's a personal friend, you can ask them if they really meant to block you – but you won't be able to do it with Twitter.

Twitter has suspended my account because I have allegedly broken a rule by tweeting too much or following too many people. My account won't be reinstated until I promise not to break the rule again. What's going on? I don't even know what exactly I'm supposed to have done wrong, or what the rule is, so how can I promise not to do it again?

Chill. This happens to many people, especially when they've just started on Twitter. Apparently, Twitter has severe limits for new users, and if you're very active, Twitter treats you as a suspected spammer. It's frustrating that Twitter doesn't tell you what exactly you've done wrong, or how many people you may follow and how many tweets you may post – but if you simply confirm that you won't break the rule, the problem goes away. For the next few days, use Twitter sparingly, and after that, you can pretty much do what you like (at least until the day you hit the 2K barrier).

Why does Twitter impose these weird limits? And why does Twitter not tell us what exactly the limits are and what's required to overcome them?

The limits – including that much-hated 2K barrier - are intended to keep automated accounts and spam bots down. Perhaps it works for this, but it also turns off genuine users.

The reason Twitter doesn't reveal the rules and algorithms is so that the spammers can't write a programme to overcome them.

It's frustrating, but not a big deal. If you hit a limit, just wait a day (or even just half an hour) and you can tweet again. If Twitter demands an assurance that you won't repeat an offence, give that assurance, even if you don't understand what your offence was.

As a general guideline, aim for a maximum of 1,000 tweets and following no more than 1,000 people per day, although the limits vary, and tend to be lower for new users.

The 2,000 followings barrier is the only limit that's a serious problem, and Chapter 24 shows how you can overcome this.

I see you're always helping people on Twitter, answering their questions, showing them how to do things Aren't you worried that someone will exploit it? Where do you draw the line?

I enjoy helping people, and if it can be done in 140 characters, I usually do it.

Of course, some people expect a lot more. They request that I read their novel, and critique/review/endorse it. I don't do that. If I follow someone, it's because I'm willing to read their 140 character tweets – not their 100,000-word novels, their blogs and everything else.

Some presume that because I follow them, they have a right to my time. If I don't answer a question immediately, if I'm not available to chat when they fancy it, and if I'm not at their beck and call 24 hours a day they get stroppy. Oh, and some expect me to be their private writing coach, giving them personal instruction and feedback outside Twitter.

I ignore such demands, or reply simply. *Sorry, I don't have the time.*

Which other books are part of the *Writer's Craft* series? Are more books in the pipeline?

Published so far: *Writing Fight Scenes, Writing Scary Scenes, The Word-Loss Diet, Writing About Magic, Writing About Villains, Writing Dark Stories, Writing Short Stories to Promote Your Novels, Twitter for Writers.*

Many more are in the pipeline.

You tweet a lot about Sulu the Cat. Is he real?

Oh yes, he is very real, a little black tom whom I adopted from the cat rescue shelter. He's sweet and bright, and he has an uncanny affinity for Twitter. Other cats simply sit on the keyboard. Mine tweets – typing either simultaneously with me, or on his own when my back is turned.

Here's one of his recent tweets: '''*44MMMMMMMMMM?*

When I try to write a book, he opens the Twitter tab. I've even caught him checking the currently trending topics. I think he waits for #Sulu #Cat to become a worldwide trend.

Who did the cover art for this book?

Erica Syverson. She has painted many book covers for me, including the others in the *Writer's Craft* series, the *Six Scary Tales* series, *Bites: Ten Tales of Vampires*, *Haunted: Ten Tales of Ghosts*, *Undead: Ten Tales of Zombies* and (in collaboration with Paul Davies) *Storm Dancer*.

Will you also write a book *Facebook for Writers*?

Sorry, no. I don't understand Facebook well enough.

Besides Twitter, what other social networks do you use?

Twitter is my main social network, the one where I'm most active. I also use others, but on a smaller scale:

Facebook
https://www.facebook.com/RayneHallAuthor
Google+
https://plus.google.com/b/111533929774901928409/1115
33929774901928409/posts/p/pub
DeviantArt http://RayneHall.deviantart.com/
GoodReads
https://www.goodreads.com/author/show/4451266.Ray
ne_Hall
BookLikes http://RayneHall.booklikes.com/
Pinterest http://www.pinterest.com/RayneHallauthor

I simply don't have the time to do every social network thoroughly. After all, I have a life to live and books to write.

CHAPTER 37: GLOSSARY

App = 'Application' = a programme offering Twitter-related features

Avatar = Profile picture

Block = Preventing someone from reading your tweets and from bothering you

Cyber-bully = A person who pursues and abuses vulnerable people, often by assuming several identities

Direct Message = A tweet sent to one individual; nobody else can see it

Discover = The tab where Twitter suggests people to follow, tweets to read, things to do. Interesting but not necessary.

DM = Direct message

Follow = Choosing the people whose tweets you want to read

Follower = Someone who chooses to receive your tweets

Hacking = Gaining unauthorised access to someone's account (through phishing, password theft etc)

Handle = Username, starting with '@'

Hashtag = A word preceded by the '#' symbol; emphasised and easily searchable

IMO = Short for 'in my opinion, used in tweets (also IMHO = 'in my humble opinion')

List = A curated compilation of usernames, usually with a common theme

Log-in = Signing into your Twitter account

LOL = Short for 'laughing out loud' or 'lots of laughs', used in tweets

Modified Retweet = A retweet where the retweeter has added or changed something.

MT = Modified retweet (also 'MRT')

Notifications = The tab where you see only tweets addressed to you or mentioning you. Sometimes called 'Connect' or 'Interactions'

OH = Short for 'overheard', used in tweets

OTOH = Short for 'on the other hand', used in tweets

Promoted tweets = Tweets where the sender has paid Twitter for preferred placement

Protected tweets = Tweets sent by someone who chooses not to let the public see them

Retweet = Sharing someone else's tweet with your followers

Shoutout = A tweet mentioning someone in a positive way

SO = Shoutout

Spam = Unwanted promotion using aggressive, invasive methods

Timeline = The tab where you can see all the tweets sent by people you follow

Troll = A person who provokes others into anger or fights.

Tweep = Person using Twitter. (Plural 'tweeps' or 'tweeple')

Tweet = A short message on Twitter

TweetDeck = A useful app; basically an extension of Twitter. Free.

Unfollow = Stop getting someone's tweets

Update = A tweet

URL = Uniform source locator = web address, internet link

DEAR READER,

I hope you enjoyed this book and have found a lot of inspiration, ideas and practical tricks.

Choose the ones you want to apply, skip those you don't like, and modify my suggestions to suit your own strategy.

There's more to Twitter than this book covers - I've focused on what's most relevant to writers -, and Twitter adds new features all the time. Experiment, discover new things, make mistakes and learn from them.

Send me a tweet about how you got on with this book and which chapters have been most useful to you. I'll probably retweet you (but can't make promises). My Twitter is @RayneHall. You can also email me: rayne_hall_author@yahoo.com, especially if you want to tell me more than fits into 140 characters, such as suggestions for a revised edition or typos which have escaped the proofreader's eagle eyes.

If you find this book helpful, it would be great if you could spread the word about it. Maybe you know other writers who would benefit.

Reviews on sites like Amazon, Barnes & Noble, GoodReads, BookLikes, Smashwords etc are very welcome. Email me the link to your review, and I'll send you a free review copy (ebook) of one of my other Writer's Craft books. Let me know which one you would like: *Writing Fight Scenes, Writing Scary Scenes, The Word-Loss Diet, Writing About Magic, Writing About Villains, Writing Dark Stories, Writing Short Stories to Promote Your Novels.*

With best wishes for your tweeting and writing success,

Rayne Hall

Made in the USA
Coppell, TX
23 March 2020